Praise for *Get Out* (

MW01258320

"Luckman illuminates a path of alchemical transformation for healing our wounds and unlocking our full potential as conscious co-creators of reality. This empowering and inspirational book unveils the shamanic secrets to transcending the illusion of death and manifesting our highest aspirations … [R]eaders are invited to step through a magical portal beyond life's apparent boundaries and embark on the ultimate hero's journey—a profound inward adventure toward self-realization and spiritual freedom." —David Jay Brown, author, *Dreaming Wide Awake*

"The Hero of a Thousand Red Pills, Sol Luckman has had an invaluable influence on awakening consciousness and dispelling false realities. *Get Out of Here Alive* is a rewarding and useful map for the hero's journey." —Miguel Conner, author, *The Occult Elvis*

"Weaving together threads of esoteric wisdom, cutting-edge science, and transformative spiritual practices, Luckman offers a revolutionary blueprint for transcending the boundaries of mortality […] This book is not merely a guide—it's a conversation with the cosmos, an invitation to unlock your highest potential, and a masterclass in the art of becoming more than human." —Laurence Galian, author, *Alien Parasites*

"This work stands out for anyone who needs a new outlook on modern life and technology or wants a guided method for self-introspection." —Entrada Publishing

"In his inimitable way, Sol shows how to better understand and navigate our way through 'reality' via a synthesis of quantum physics, alchemy, shamanism, and literature. This, in turn, leads us to recognize that we are actually tricked into living a certain way […] Fortunately, Sol also offers us solutions, sharing exercises and activities we can use to protect ourselves and our energy […] An excellent, mind-expanding book." —Dawn Lester, coauthor, *What Really Makes You Ill?*

"There is a lot to unpack in this book; its innate positivity and many included useful references and techniques offer neophytes and the more experienced traveller some useful insights, while encouraging your own experimentation and individuality. Sol beautifully weaves a plethora of concepts and authors into a complex but achievable journey of inner-space growth." —William Bullock, Certified Clinical Hypnotherapist

"I highly recommend this book to all fellow consciousness explorers! It's excellent and will challenge and encourage you. I was encouraged and will be contemplating the wealth of information shared for a long time. I love the practicality and usefulness of the information." —April Novoa, author, *Love Is, Fear Is Not*

"This book is a powerful reminder to break free from the distractions and to start honoring what truly nourishes us. It's a call to wake up, to stop feeding into the chaos, and to reclaim our power—the power to choose what we create and to rise above the noise of the easily manipulated, outer-influenced brain work. Don't get lost in the noise of the mechanical operating system brain—learn what it means to become the shaman who fearlessly goes inward." —Shan Beaste, Sound Healing Therapist

ALSO BY SOL LUCKMAN

FICTION

Cali the Destroyer

Snooze: A Story of Awakening

NONFICTION

The World Cult & You: Your Place in It & Your Way Out of It

Playing in the MAGIC: How to Manifest Whatever You Desire in the Simulation

Potentiate Your DNA: A Practical Guide to Healing & Transformation with the Regenetics Method

Conscious Healing: Book One on the Regenetics Method

HUMOR

The Angel's Dictionary: A Spirited Glossary for the Little Devil in You

MEMOIR

Musings from a Small Island: Everything under the Sun

GET OUT OF HERE
ALVE

Inner Alchemy & Immortality

SOL LUCKMAN

Copyright © 2025 by Sol Luckman. All Rights Reserved.

ISBN: 978-1-7369595-9-6
Library of Congress Number: 2024922630

First Edition 2025
Crow Rising Transformational Media
Hilton Head Island, South Carolina
www.crowrising.com

No part of this book may be reproduced in any form or by any electronic or mechanical means, including information storage and retrieval systems, without permission in writing from the author, except by a reviewer, who has the option to quote brief passages in a review.

For paperback, ebook and audiobook versions of *Get Out of Here Alive*, visit **www.solluckman.com**.

Disclaimer: This is a work of opinion and is in no way intended to provide medical advice, diagnosis, treatment, promises, or guarantees. Consult your healthcare provider before taking action regarding any information relative to health or mental health presented herein.

CONTENTS

For my fellow Riders on the Storm

PREFACE

Thank you for getting off the beaten track enough to join me in entertaining—in a completely nondogmatic way—the admittedly radical possibility that death doesn't have to be the end of life's journey.

I realize this is a hefty proposition and that extraordinary claims require extraordinary support. I can only hope that you find in these pages the inspiration and tools to stop looking *outward* for proof of important things (if you haven't already) and start (or continue) looking *inward* to decide for yourself if my concepts have merit.

This book is especially for anyone who already qualifies as—or is open to becoming—a freethinker, defined by *Merriam-Webster* as "one who forms opinions on the basis of reason independently of authority." I'd only add that, in my dictionary, freethinking also involves, wherever possible, experientially trying on a concept before intellectually judging it.

With that in mind, and with philosophical wrangling over mortality's inevitability aside, if you're willing to implement just some of the many empowering strategies and techniques herein, my sincere expectation is that your overall mind-body-spirit health will improve in obvious and even tangible ways, large and small.

If you do derive benefit from (or otherwise wish to weigh in on) this book, I welcome your honest feedback in the form of a review and rating on Amazon, Goodreads, BookBub, and wherever else *Get Out of Here Alive* is sold that works for you.

I also invite you to subscribe for free to my expanding self-help library for freethinkers, consciousness explorers and wellness aficionados at **solluckman.substack.com**. There, with a complimentary 7-day trial, you'll have access to all my officially published books and some exclusive ones besides (and where available, their audio versions, including the audiobook of this text).

Additionally on that website, I've begun sharing a series of original exercises called PragmAlchemy for engaging in practical inner alchemy. If you're interested in taking your energy and focus to the next level, with ease and grace and some restorative self-bodywork added to the mix, you can seamlessly integrate these activities into your daily routine.

Please accept my sincere gratitude once again for reading and contemplating the following chapters. Rest assured they build up to quite a stunning and inspirational denouement, so be sure to ride this ride all the way to the end!

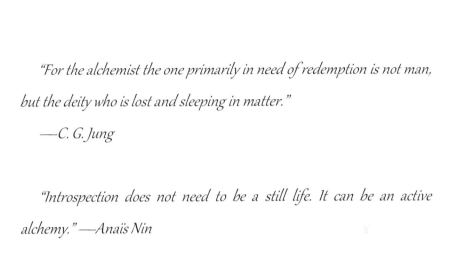

"For the alchemist the one primarily in need of redemption is not man, but the deity who is lost and sleeping in matter."

—C. G. Jung

"Introspection does not need to be a still life. It can be an active alchemy." —Anaïs Nin

"Death is the midwife of very great things ... It brings about the birth and rebirth of forms a thousand times improved."

—Paracelsus

INTRODUCTION

R.I.P. ... *Death?*

Opening the Doors of Perception

It's hardly surprising that one of the most iconic and bestselling musician biographies of all time, and the first (of a veritable "Spanish Caravan") written about the Doors front man Jim Morrison, was titled *No One Here Gets Out Alive*.

The lyric is a line from "Five to One," a perennial fan favorite penned by Morrison but credited officially to the Doors—and it has stuck in my mind (as it has in countless others over more than half a century since its 1968 release) like a splinter, to reference the movie *The Matrix* that also figures prominently in this book.

When I was living in Paris in the early 1990s, I became obsessed with Morrison, and not just his music but his often macabre poetry as well. This was shortly after the release of Oliver Stone's uber provocative rock biopic that put to shame all other rock biopics, *The Doors*.

As a birthday present, my girlfriend gave me a bilingual copy of *The Lords & the New Creatures*, Morrison's first volume of poetry replete with dark meditations on sex, celebrity, drugs, and (of course) death.

While riding the Metro, sitting on the steps of Montmartre and sipping espresso at cafés, I found myself reading it alternately in English and the French translation to capture more and more nuances of Morrison's cryptic, multilayered thought.

Jim had died in Paris and was buried in the city's famously lovely necropolis, Père Lachaise Cemetery. His grave — which once featured a stone bust with his big hippy hair made by a Croatian sculptor and stolen in 1988 — was, and still is, a literal shrine to many tourists, fans and hipster locals making rock 'n' roll pilgrimages from near and far.

Practically as controversial in death as in life, ever since his untimely demise in 1971 that rocked the rock world, Morrison has lingered in a sort of public half-life.

Simultaneously, he has been an inspiration for counterculture and music lovers; a nuisance for Parisians fed up with the incessant drinking, smoking and carousing that have turned his grave into an eternal party; and a would-be prodigal son to his home country, where a Florida politician bizarrely (and unsuccessfully) sought to have Jim's final resting place relocated to his birthplace, the Space Coast!

My girlfriend — call her Kate — and I regularly visited Morrison's final resting place, and often partook in the festivities, which I must admit were exemplary displays of Dionysian behavior … if inevitably a regretted hangover source.

Filled with more cemeteries, church crypts and bone-lined Catacombs than you could shake a Gauloise at, Paris invited an ongoing meditation on the afterlife. Like *Harry Potter*'s Myrtle without the moaning, I regularly found myself contemplating the seeming inevitability of death.

And then one overcast Parisian winter afternoon half a decade later, when I was back in town visiting a new girlfriend, while standing in front of Morrison's grave strewn with flowers and cigarette butts yet again as if no time had elapsed and nothing had changed, the doors of my perception (hat tip to William Blake and Aldous Huxley) suddenly burst wide open when a still small voice inside me asked this simply disarming question:

"Does no one here get out alive?"

Might There Be an Alternative to Death?

That splinter of a question would ever after irritate my gray matter with a curious itch I couldn't scratch.

Known as the Lizard King, a double-edged epithet if ever there was one, Morrison was infamous for his fascination with all things shamanic and mystical, an interest that undoubtedly informed his own obsession with mortality.

Not long after my last visit to Paris, suffering from a mysterious and debilitating autoimmune illness with elements of chronic fatigue and fibromyalgia, I embarked on my own healing journey through the valley of the shadow of death.

I've written extensively about this "shamanic" phase of mine in my second book on the Regenetics Method, *Potentiate Your DNA*. Regenetics is a powerful sound healing technique that ultimately restored my health that I developed with my life partner, Leigh. I'll have a great deal more to say about this work in relation to the critically important subject of energy preservation and cultivation in a later chapter.

During this transformational period, as I sought to heal my wounded body, mind and spirit, I began extensively studying shamanism, mysticism, alchemy, physics, epigenetics, and many other disciplines. This information slowly but surely wove itself together into a very different conceptual fabric from the comparatively more "normie" one to which I was accustomed.

Out of this novel inner tapestry emerged my initial book on Regenetics, *Conscious Healing*, in which I first examined the "fringe" notion that there might just be an alternative to death and dying.

In my most recent book, *The World Cult & You: Your Place in It & Your Way Out of It*, in which Regenetics played a comparatively minor role, my questioning of death's unavoidability went even deeper.

This book you're reading is a continuation of that examination with a new and vastly expanded emphasis on shamanic and alchemical concepts and processes that have everything to do with the most straightforward—and maybe *only*—way of getting out of here alive.

I'll clarify exactly what I mean by "alive" in due course. Trust me, it's pretty cool, even if it may not be exactly what you expect. For the time being, let me assure you that the territory I'll cover offers an absolutely fascinating vista into the Undiscovered Country of the beyond.

Long before discussing the ultimate (and optional) Hero's Journey into the Great Unknown, however, the material I'll be sharing through much of this book is designed to improve your life today in a myriad of subtle and not-so-subtle ways—even as your consciousness is prepped for much greater possibilities of worldly transcendence.

What *Is* This Place?

Before we go further into a discussion of getting out of here, let's take a moment to define what is meant by "here." What is the nature of this confusing way station between birth and (usually) death accompanied by obliteration of identity we call home?

Planet, plane, simulation, hallucination, hell, heaven on earth … The hypotheses as to this realm's true character are as many as there are bored conspiracy theorists tapping away on crusty laptops in their parents' basements.

But what if the childishly simple answer to our conundrum is given away in this aphorism popularized in "Row Row Row Your Boat": "Life is but a dream"?

In the world of adult literature, perhaps Edgar Allen Poe phrased it best:

All that we see or seem
Is but a dream within a dream.

Poe's haunting poem has long acted like yet another splinter aggravating my mind, challenging my accepted notions of this Matrix-like "reality." Are we truly awake while experiencing the tangible world around us? Or are we adrift in a dream flux of illusions, our senses hoodwinking us at every turn?

The boundary between dreams and reality gets muddy indeed when we consider the nature of our perceptions. Our senses, those windows to the world, are far from perfect instruments that are extremely susceptible to manipulation and misinterpretation. What we perceive as unquestionably solid and real could be nothing more than smoke and mirrors, projections of our own psyches.

The very act of doubting our reality indicates a flicker of suspicion, a seed of uncertainty germinating in our subconscious. Perhaps this nagging sense of unease, this wondering if something isn't altogether as it should be, is a clue, a whisper from the wellspring of our being that there's more to this existence than meets the eye.

Imagine for a moment that our waking life is truly but a dream, a meticulously crafted simulation of sorts designed to test the limits of our perception and self-awareness.

What if the world we inhabit—with all its confounding complexities and contradictions—is nothing more than an elaborate stage set, a grand illusion orchestrated by a poorly understood force? If this were true, how could we possibly know for certain? What signs or signals might betray the actual nature of our world and our place in it?

The answer, perhaps, lies in the anomalies, the glitches in the Matrix, those bizarre instances when the veil of perception momentarily slips and we catch a glimpse of the machinery behind reality's curtain.

A sudden sense of *déjà vu*, a feeling of being secretly observed, a recurring dream that seems eerily factual. What if these aren't the misfirings of our own warped brains, random occurrences with no deeper meaning? What if they're actually subtle hints, whispers from the multiverse urging us to question our reality?

The trope of reality as an illusion definitely isn't a modern development. Philosophers and writers throughout history have endeavored to crack this tough nut, relentlessly probing the nature of existence and the limits of human perception.

Plato's allegory of the cave, for example, compares us to prisoners relegated to an abyss, mistaking shadows on the wall for the real thing. Similarly, René Descartes' famous dictum, "I think, therefore I am," highlights the fundamental problem of certainty.

If our senses can so easily deceive us, how can we be confident in our understanding of anything, even our own physical existence?

Literature, too, is replete with stories of characters who question their sanity, their grasp on reality maddeningly unraveling as they delve deeper into the mysteries of their own tormented minds. From Poe's spooky tales to the psychological thrillers of modern fiction, the theme of dream versus reality continues to rivet and disturb.

If we're indeed, like Neo in *The Matrix*, "living in a dream world," the inevitable questions then become:

Can we wake up?

If so, how do we wake up?

What exactly awaits us if and when we do wake up?

The possibility of waking up from (or even *in*) the dream offers a glimmer of hope, a sense that there's more to existence than this mundane rat race. It suggests that we're not just NPCs, non-player characters in a preprogrammed reality—but that, instead, we're capable of becoming truly conscious players with the power to shape our own destinies.

Out through the In Door

Shamanism and inner alchemy offer some of the most empowering strategies for freethinkers and other free spirits interested in "waking up" enough to craft their own storyline and direct their own fate.

Not surprisingly, both disciplines firmly agree with what I've been saying in my own related work for some time now: *the only way out is in.*

To reverse the title of another iconic rock masterpiece, this one by Led Zeppelin of "Stairway to Heaven" fame, we can say without reservation that to exit the Matrix of this dreamscape, we must go *out through the in door.*

Energetically speaking, this statement is meant to be taken almost literally. To transcend this place, whatever, wherever and whenever it is, we must first travel *inward* through the wrinkles and folds of our own conscious, subconscious and unconscious minds.

In doing so while utilizing specific techniques I'll outline, it's possible to amass enough energy, or personal power, to fly *outward* beyond the confines of this reality construct with our consciousness intact.

In other words, though there are no guarantees in life (or death), we at least have a shot—a fool's chance maybe but a shot nevertheless—at getting out of here alive.

I get that some readers of a skeptical or cynical bent will find the notion of cheating death and becoming immortal nothing but fool's gold. To whom I say if you're going to be a fool, you'd better do it right.

Being a fool the right way means not being the kind of fool who uncritically accepts so-called real-world truths that attempt to explain (away) the inexplicable, while unthinkingly denying huge swaths of data that contradict those very "truths."

The wrong type of fool focuses only on the profound while sweeping the absurd under the rug. The right kind, however, realizes that "profound" and "absurd" don't exist in isolation but as a meaningful paradox at the center of human experience: the *absurdly profound*.

Shedding light on a similar subject, F. Scott Fitzgerald wrote, "The test of a first-rate intelligence is the ability to hold two opposed ideas in the mind at the same time, and still retain the ability to function."

For anyone desiring to go beyond this world's illusory limits, the most important thing is to avoid accepting anything anyone (including yours truly) asserts as "fact" without personally testing it with an open mind … and heart.

I encourage you to—at least as an experiment—stop listening to the mouthpieces of the world and see for yourself whether my words have any substance. That means getting in touch with your inner shaman and committing to alchemically transforming the lead of your current diminished reality into the gold of your total expansive self.

Even if, heaven forbid, you fail in your attempt to blow this popsicle stand while giving a single finger salute to the Grim Reaper, the lifestyle recommendations, thought experiments and energy-enhancing protocols I share in this book can dramatically improve your quality of life during whatever time you have left.

This upgrade can include rejuvenation, increased energy, a better mental outlook, more balanced emotions, greater abundance, a renewed sense of purpose, and even physical healing.

So what are we waiting for? Onward and inward!

CHAPTER ONE

The Hero's Journey past the Dragon, through the Shadow & into the Dark Sea of Awareness

"Stop acting so small. You are the universe in ecstatic motion." —*Rumi*

The Quantum Dance

The world appears substantial. We bump into things and each other. We feel the rain and would swear on our mother's grave we're encountering a collection of material drops. To say otherwise invites cynical laughter and derision.

Yet quantum physics, the study of the universe at its most minute level, unveils a startlingly different picture from what today's hyper-materialist humans so glibly dub reality.

This may be old hat to some, but in the quantum realm, the things we take for granted aren't really *things* at all. In other words, they're not solid. There is—to adapt a phrase I adore and often cite attributed to Gertrude Stein—simply *no there there.*

Even those of us who understand some of the scientific theories behind this concept often only pay lip service to it — believing one thing (reality isn't solid) while acting with cognitive dissonance based on a diametrically opposed belief (reality is hard and immutable).

Nevertheless, it can be shown, intuited and eventually even seen with the inner senses that this world is nothing more or less than an intricate dance of energy, a sea of swirling possibilities where everything is constantly in flux.

Seers and mystics, in fact, sometimes refer to this foundational realm out of which the movie of our lives momentarily projects as the *Dark Sea of Awareness* — a term I first encountered in the shamanic work of Carlos Castaneda and which has more recently informed John Kreiter's groundbreaking contemporary revelation of the ancient mysteries of alchemy.

Atoms, the building blocks of so-called matter, however much they might seem to be physically circumscribed, aren't actually like tiny billiard balls. That's kindergarten science.

From a shamanic or alchemical perspective, atoms are more like sentient waves, their intelligently responsive existence a blur of potential until they magically appear to materialize.

Mimetic Desire & Belief Manipulation

There is, of course, a method to the multiverse's creative madness, an order and energetic methodology behind what appears to be pure chaos. From a human perspective, as Kreiter observes in *The Magnum Opus,*

Beliefs are the underlying structures that shape our lives [...] They create and give direction to thoughts and ideas, and these thoughts trigger or induce emotions that then naturally propel raw and very powerful energy, through and around the body, and into the environment at large.

While this may sound all well and good, there's a sobering pitfall to the way we go about imagining our world.

Through a process known as "mimetic desire," which leads people to assign value based not on direct experience but through imitation of what others appear to desire, *beliefs can be conditioned and even installed in the human psyche*.

As French philosopher René Girard explained in his influential mimetic theory, "Man is the creature who does not know what to desire, and he turns to others in order to make up his mind. We desire what others desire because we imitate their desires."

The upshot is that the world brought into being by people through their (installed) belief systems can be manipulated by anyone—or *anything*—powerful and knowledgeable enough to pull the right emotional strings to produce ... the desired beliefs!

In my previous book, *The World Cult & You*, I spent a lot of time on the subject of what some have called the "tyranny of belief." This phrase can refer to the control and manipulation of the human herd through society-wide implementation of both laughably obvious and cleverly camouflaged forms of indoctrination.

To use George Orwell's famous term, we're talking about *groupthink*, which Wikipedia describes as a psychological phenomenon that occurs within a group of people in which the desire for harmony or conformity in the group results in ... irrational or dysfunctional decision-making .... [T]he desire for cohesiveness in a group may produce a tendency among its members to agree at all costs. This causes the group to minimize conflict and reach a consensus decision without critical evaluation.

The key takeaway is that society's members are psychically pressured into defining "true" and "right" based not on personal experience or direct gnosis (inner knowing), but on what the creators of social discourse put forward as "true" and "right"—in other words, what to believe in— even in the absence of genuine logic or compelling evidence.

This situation leads—almost inevitably, it would seem— to the creation of a certain kind of top-down, pyramidal structure that controls society, culture and, given enough free rein, eventually the world itself.

I'll return to the massively important (and almost completely ignored, due to social engineering) topic of mental "reality installations" a bit later. But for now, let's observe ...

The Observer Effect

The oft-discussed "observer effect" based on the so-called particle-wave duality made famous by numerous researchers conducting double-slit experiments isn't a negligible phenomenon.

To the contrary, the observer effect applies to far more than just photons appearing as particles or waves depending on whether an observer happens to be around to coalesce them with the power of attention.

Doing this with light is just a cheap party trick, like pulling a rabbit (a particle) out of the infinite probability waves of the quantum soup (the Dark Sea of Awareness). But things can get way more … intriguing.

As evidenced by such minutely scrutinized paranormal phenomena as tulpas and egregores, the really jaw-dropping magic happens when — knowingly or otherwise — we use our focus to collapse waves into actual "matter."

A notion deriving from Tibetan Buddhism, a tulpa is said to be a thoughtform materialization, often taking human shape and serving as a helper or "servitor," generated by way of consistently applied intention and attention.

Similarly, an egregore, we read in Wikipedia, is a "non-physical entity that arises from the collective thoughts of a distinct group of people … [T]he concept has referred to a psychic manifestation, or a thoughtform, which occurs when any group shares a common motivation — being made up of, and influencing, the thoughts of the group."

Leaving aside the many connections between such thoughtforms and reality installations that form and inform groupthink and related behaviors, let's cut to the chase about the larger implications of such phenomena.

Not to put too fine a point on it, but the documented existence of tulpas and egregores (both of which have often been witnessed by multiple individuals simultaneously) strongly suggests, in Jon Rappoport's emphatic words, that "THE UNIVERSE [IS] A PRODUCT OF MIND."

Indeed, one could argue that the observer effect is the primary energetic dynamic of "reality" itself.

This effect showcases the eminently malleable nature of the LEGO pieces of our world—atoms—as material objects that appear to become so only through an act of creative focus. This may strain credulity, but at the fundamental level of energy, it's just how "things" are.

The human gaze is so potent, in fact, it can actually be felt with our sixth sense (what I think of as the psychic one), as biochemist Rupert Sheldrake redundantly demonstrates in *The Sense of Being Stared At*.

Mind over Matter

The observer effect puts our everyday perceptions and assumptions in a blender. It dictates—if we're to be honest with ourselves, sober in our thinking, and not reactionary in our emotions—that *the world we see is NOT the ultimate reality, but merely a projection of it.*

From this perspective the manifest world is revealed as what Hindu mystics referred to as *maya*, illusion, the imaginal outpourings of minds—like children naturally playing in magical constructs that seem eminently real—simply doing what minds do.

In the words of physicist Arthur Stanley Eddington, "The mind-stuff of the world is, of course, something more general than our individual conscious minds … It is difficult for the matter-of-fact physicist to accept the view that the substratum of everything is of mental character. But no one can deny that mind is the first and most direct thing in our experience, and all else is remote inference."

Contrary to the dogma downloaded from our many cult-like institutions of higher (actually lower) learning, we're not in any way separate from this quantum dance of the imagination; we're inextricably bound up in it. In a mind-melting paradox, we somehow manage to give rise to the quantum dance ... even as it dances us!

We're like the mythical ouroboros, the serpent consuming its own tail, a stylized image of which I've placed at the end of each chapter herein to remind us of our absurdly profound and infinite nature.

As we learn to appreciate the waltz of shadows on the walls of Plato's cave, we begin to grasp that the solid "objects" we think of as ourselves are merely illusions moving through a greater illusion.

Only then can we begin to *get real*—as it slowly dawns on us that objectivity is a subjective fantasy implanted in us by an external will seeking to curtail our creativity by limiting our minds to our own detriment.

As I mentioned in the Introduction, it's possible to become so "real," so energetically sovereign, so full of power and magic that we can grow wings—figuratively anyway—and fly this chicken coop.

In other words, we can leave this delusional world (and the World Cult that sustains it) flapping in the breeze while exiting as increasingly self-realized beings.

Few will even attempt this feat of alchemical transmutation, I realize. But at the very least, we can get real in our understanding—or better, innerstanding—as we begin to collect the scattered fragments of ourselves we've left behind in our unconsciousness.

As I'll discuss in due course, shamanic recapitulation, inner alchemy and my own powerful form of "ener-genetic" work, the Regenetics Method, are extremely useful tools in this internal process of awakening and perhaps eventually becoming our whole, authentic selves.

A critical piece of this holistic self-becoming involves the deeply felt realization that our thoughts, beliefs and intentions aren't merely mental or "just imaginary" events. On the contrary, they're potent forces interacting synergistically with the quantum field, the biofield of the Universal Mind, if you will.

In a culture crafted by eager yes-men and -women to an overbearing materialism, this may be a hard pill to swallow. But that doesn't change this clear (to many anyway) dynamic: *the simply powerful act of observation influences the universe at its most basic level.*

How *far* does this go? Might it go *all the way*? Could it be not just a micro but a *macro* effect as well? I think so.

What we focus on, what we believe, has a direct effect on the unfolding of actual events—small ones, yes, but large ones as well. Indeed, our sustained focus is the primary driver in bringing what are initially purely imagined scenarios (some on an expanded scale) to life.

At the micro end of the spectrum, this even applies to our genes. These can be switched on and off consciously through intentional application of our awareness, as Dr. Bruce Lipton has shown in his inspiring research in the emerging science of epigenetics.

Epigenetics reveals that your body isn't a genetically predetermined flesh robot, but is regulated by a set of gene switches that can be turned on or off—by you—mindfully. Ergo, our genes aren't our destiny. We have far more control over their expression than most ever imagined.

This isn't mere philosophical musing we're engaging in here. Epigenetic effects are strongly backed by experiments—repeated ones in many cases—which show its great power to improve health and wellbeing through the exercise of conscious intention and attention.

Whether we like it or not, we're walking placebo and nocebo generators, able to create health miracles or disasters (usually without even realizing we're the ones doing so) practically in the blink of an eye.

Change Is an Inside Job

Meanwhile, looking around us at the social landscape, it could hardly be more apparent that history is a sad testament to the limitations of external change, or changing things from the outside.

A dime a dozen and almost invariably overrated in hindsight, countless revolutions, insurgencies, wars, conflicts, struggles and social movements have stubbornly—and blindly—sought to create a better world.

Yet true, lasting transformation remains elusive at the groupthink level. We grapple with the same issues, generation after generation, in this hamster wheel called "reality." Why is external change so damn challenging?

Because, I contend, to echo Henry David Thoreau's celebrated quote about the branches and roots of evil, pursuing external change only addresses symptoms, not the deeper cause.

The world we see "out there" is a reflection of our cleverly molded shared consciousness, our collective belief installed through manipulation of our mimetic desire, not a given "thing" that can't be changed. This means, as in the adage, that we can heal the world only if we heal ourselves.

By succumbing to external conditioning and looking *outside* ourselves for answers, thus denying the power of our imagination and ignoring the only viable path forward into the future (that of *internal* transformation), we're bound to just keep pouring gasoline on a world already on fire.

As Carl Jung wisely observed in his meditations on the shadow, "Whatever is rejected from the self appears in the world as an event."

The world can most definitely be changed, but not by using the materialist ways we've been taught designed to keep us beating our heads against the walls and bars of the "real world."

To change this designedly dysfunctional construct, which our own co-opted creative attention is actually responsible for materializing and maintaining, we must first change *ourselves*.

Neville Goddard, a true pioneer of creative consciousness, said it best:

> Stop trying to change the world since it is only the mirror. Man's attempt to change the world by force is as fruitless as breaking a mirror in the hope of changing his face. Leave the mirror and change your face. Leave the world alone and change your conceptions of yourself. The reflection then will be satisfactory.

We must, then, shift our perceptions, beliefs, intentions, and emotions. We must harness the power of the observer effect to induce a quantum change in the observed world. We must return to our center and resurrect our innate ability to perform miracles with only the tool of our consciousness.

This is true magic, not something out of Hogwarts. We're more than capable of waving our wands over the manifest world and making its madness disappear. But first, we have to realize that we're born wizards, each and every one of us. There are no Muggles here.

The Hero's Journey

Another movie that provides a powerful metaphor for this book, as mentioned, is *The Matrix*. I'm referencing in particular the first installment of this franchise, whose liberating message appeared to have been—as typically happens—doomed from the start to be hijacked by its follow-ups crawling with hidden agendas.

Neo's iconic story in the first movie depicts a world where reality is a computer simulation, a prison for the mind. The characters must choose to take the blue pill and remain in blissful ignorance or swallow the red one and face the truth, however unsettling. (If you're unaware of this famous plotline that has inspired a million memes, you obviously took the blue pill!)

We, too, live in a sort of Matrix—one of our own manipulated mental making. Here it's worth repeating that our emotions, thoughts and beliefs are the raw power that can be focused to create our experience of reality.

To begin breaking free (individually before even so much as contemplating doing this collectively), we must stop taking the black pill of skepticism and down the red pill of introspection. Only then, by exercising our will, can we resist the temptation to deny our true potential using the blue pill and, instead, graduate to the white pill of transcendence.

Less poetically, our task is to confront the limitations of our own belief systems, and the resultant intellectual constructs, and dismantle the bars and wires of our self-imposed prison. To do this requires looking *inside* as responsible agents of change, not *outside* as victims of a world beyond our control.

The Hero's Journey, a narrative archetype found in myths and stories across cultures popularized by comparative mythologist Joseph Campbell, provides a roadmap for this inner transformation.

The heroic quest typically highlights a seemingly average person (think Thomas Anderson before he becomes Neo) who embarks on a perilous undertaking, confronts challenges and temptations, and ultimately returns to his or her starting place, transformed and usually upgraded.

This myth appears central to human experience. The Tarot, for example, which reads as a distillation of ancient mythology, is in essence about the heroic quest to become one's true self. Even the parable of the Prodigal Son can be interpreted as a retelling of the Hero's Journey.

As you might expect by now, this journey isn't merely external; it's primarily internal. The Hero's Journey, applied to our *Matrix* analogy, suggests that the only way *out* of the so-called simulation is *into* oneself.

The hero's ultimate inner battle is against the enemy within, the shadow self, our own Agent Smith, the unrecognized and unintegrated aspects of the psyche that only battle and hinder us until we make peace with them.

There's also the small matter of a dangerous Dragon—a literal monster—guarding the entrance to our internal cave which we must face and defeat to achieve liberation from the Matrix. But more on that later.

By standing up to our fears, examining our darkness and reassembling our fragmented selves, we undergo a profound metamorphosis ... provided we're up to the challenge of seeing the world for what it is: a product of our own projections that have been manipulated for something else's benefit.

As we embark on this challenging yet transformational inner journey, we tap into the quantum self, the infinite potential that resides within. We come to realize that we're not victims of circumstance, but conscious creators with the power to literally change the world ... or at least *our* world ... by altering our worldview.

Our own reclaimed beliefs—which are more like deep knowings based on direct personal experience instead of mimetic desire—are some of the primary tools that we employ as increasingly conscious architects of our own experience.

By cultivating awareness while following our bliss and learning to work with and eventually see the energy of the Dark Sea of Awareness, and aligning our intentions with our most absurdly profound gnosis of how the universe actually works and where we fit into it, we become powerful change agents indeed.

As David Hawkins demonstrated in *Power vs. Force*, we influence the quantum field not through force, but through purposeful conscious resonance with All That Is, including all that we are.

The Hero's Journey is, in the final analysis, the shaman's, the alchemist's, the wizard's—and it's all about energy. Power up and hold on tight as you transform into more and more of the miraculous creature you've always been.

In the immortal words of W. B. Yeats, "The world is full of magic things, patiently waiting for your senses to grow sharper."

As we become more energetically empowered, we transmute into living embodiments of the world we wish to see—radiating our signature creative passions into the fabric of existence ... and inviting a new and better expression of that fabric in the here and now.

Thank you for walking beside me as I share various methods to engage and succeed in your own Hero's Journey. We'll examine everything from simplicity and dancing to the nature of the Dragon, the shadow, and the infinite world of possibilities awaiting our exploration ... beyond.

CHAPTER TWO

What Do You Have to Show for Your Life?

"Anything you cannot relinquish when it has outlived its usefulness, possesses you. And in this materialistic age, a great many of us are possessed by our possessions." —Peace Pilgrim

Complexity Is the Simplicity Killer

Are you one of those people who crave to drink so deeply of life, to suck all its marrow out, to use Thoreau's mouthwatering phrasing, that you run around like a headless chicken dying of thirst in a spiritual desert?

Are you aware of the energetic nature of all you choose to experience—how it impacts you and, daily, shapes the course of your life—or do you feel that someone or something else is secretly directing you, perhaps even covertly draining your vital force?

There are many pandemics in today's world, some less purely imaginary than others, and of these the pathological need for ever-increasing complexity nears the top of the list.

Are apps here to make life simpler or more complicated? Are you working remotely or being worked remotely? Who's in control here—you or forces seemingly beyond your control?

"Fear is the mind-killer," Frank Herbert famously wrote in *Dune*. He might also have truthfully stated that *complexity is the simplicity-killer*. Which is a crying shame because simplicity—absent any other changes in our way of life— can be a bona fide lucky charm for longevity and good health.

Contrary to the indoctrinated notion that reducing existence to the essentials is for half-wits and losers in this golden age of technological "progress," simplicity isn't simplistic—or at least it doesn't have to be.

Simplicity can be a sophisticated lifestyle choice, the result of a decision to "turn on, tune in, drop out." This famous turn of phrase by Harvard psychologist and countercultural icon Timothy Leary—called by President Richard Nixon "the most dangerous man in America" for his advocacy of psychedelics—infamously reimagined Thoreau's comparatively domesticated meme of marching to the beat of one's own drummer.

In one form or another, whether approached conservatively or with a more radical edge, simplicity is nonnegotiable. It's basically a requirement for those desiring to undertake the inner Hero's Journey of shadow work in order to move beyond the mimetic mind control of the Dragon into the limitless creative possibilities of the Dark Sea of Awareness.

Think about it. How can you expect to go *in*, where thorough and lasting change can only happen, if you're always busy chasing loose and fake change *outside* yourself in the quote-unquote "real world"?

My advice may seem like tough love, but the only solution I can see is to stop making your life so bustling and byzantine, so frantic and fragmented. Find time as often as possible to simply *stop everything*.

By doing so on a regular basis, you might even be able to "stop the world," to borrow a well-known concept from Carlos Castaneda, in order to perceive the true quantum REALITY behind "physical reality" directly.

In terms of shamanic or alchemical transformation, if you're always obsessed about something *out* there, you'll never become anything *in* there where it actually counts. As for getting out of here alive when you're up to your eyeballs following the Dragon's breadcrumb trail of empty distractions, forget it.

The Road Less Traveled

You know you've lost your simplicity when you've found your busy-ness. A packed schedule is a telltale sign of decenteredness.

If you're always having to "squeeze people in," you'll be hard-pressed to get out of the kiddie pool of this construct and enter the deeper waters of the Dark Sea of Awareness.

Goal-oriented behavior is slickly marketed in this externalizing age, material success being the name of the game here in the Desert of the Real (to reference Morpheus cribbing Jean Baudrillard). All the while our personal and collective stress over "getting shit done" depletes, harms, and even kills.

But some individuals (in the true sense of having *individuated*) have learned to live magnificently without chasing the socially imposed carrot of riches and rewards with all of its collateral damage.

These people made a conscious decision to take the road less traveled, to borrow a beloved phrase from the poetry of Robert Frost, and they provided much slow food for thought for those of us likewise in the process of ditching the fast-food mentality of contemporary culture.

Born Mildred Lisette Norman and later adopting her famous moniker, Peace Pilgrim grew out of her early "flapper" phase of frenetic social engagement to become a well-known American spiritual teacher and peace activist.

The first woman to walk the full length of the Appalachian Trail in a single season, by 1964, carrying only a toothbrush, comb, pen and map, she had walked 25,000 miles to bring attention to, among other things, the lost life-giving art of simplicity in a world dying—figuratively and literally—of overcomplexity.

By today's social-media-enforced standards, she might easily be considered a simpleton. Yet how many of those sitting comfortably in virtual judgment could, or would, live such a meaningful and memorable life replete with genuine challenges large and small?

Indeed, how many of those all too happy to judge "simpletons" today could even comprehend that intentional simplicity might be a far more satisfying and enriching lifestyle than their own frenzied, narcissistic pursuit of satisfaction and wealth?

Let me be clear that I'm *not* judging desire per se. One's motivation to live simply is itself a form of desire. We can't escape desire; nor should we try to, in my opinion.

But I do wish to point out that desire, like a laser on a swivel, can be redirected from the *outside* to the *inside*—with astonishing results of a magical nature when focused on healing, transformation, and transcendence.

Thoreau Less Traveled

On the subject of excelling in the unbridled territory surrounding the cozy confines of the norm, the famous transcendentalist stands out as another titanic American "simpleton" who pairs well with Peace Pilgrim.

Many literary scholars and historians consider Thoreau to be one of America's greatest philosophers, if not writers, so I take what he had to say on one of his favorite subjects—the importance of simplicity, which to him was like the salt of the earth—with more than a grain of salt.

"I went to the woods because I wished to live deliberately," he wrote in one of the most iconic passages in Western literature, "to front only the essential facts of life, and see if I could not learn what it had to teach, and not, when I came to die, discover that I had not lived."

He continued,

> I did not wish to live what was not life, living is so dear; nor did I wish to practice resignation, unless it was quite necessary. I wanted to live deep and suck out all the marrow of life, to live so sturdily and Spartan-like as to put to rout all that was not life, to cut a broad swath and shave close, to drive life into a corner, and reduce it to its lowest terms.

How many in our busy, complex, mostly online world would, or could, write—much less undertake—such a meaningful passage? How many of those running around today with their heads on fire could even contemplate such thoughts?

Thoreau is, in his own inimitable way, describing his personal Hero's Journey beyond the illusions and distractions of this construct. His aim is to reduce life to its essential ingredients in order to study them not just artistically but also—there's not a better word for it—*scientifically*.

He definitely put his money (what little he had or needed) where his mouth was, avoiding the pitfalls of a controlling career and others' onerous expectations and whittling away nonessentials until he could live comfortably by working only a day a week.

Much of the rest of his time he spent pursuing his passion: writing. And the world is a less dark place for it, having received a major lesson from the woods at Walden as to effective ways to practice civil disobedience that would eventually inspire none other than Mahatma Gandhi and help free India from the clutches of British colonialism.

Questions Worth Asking Yourself

As children we're instructed to "live well" and strive to "be the best we can be." But we're rarely encouraged, in good faith, to contemplate—for ourselves—what living well and being our personal best actually mean for us ... as individuals.

Instead, we accept the party line. I sum that up in my forthcoming novel *Beginner's Luke: Adventure of an Imaginary Lifetime* (an ideal fictional companion to this book) as agreeing to "tick off the appointed stages one by one through midlife crisis to forced retirement to doddering senility to death without dignity."

Given the patent absurdity of the modern experiment, some paramount questions for those of us seeking to have a profound existence are:

Whom or what am I living for?

Am I living merely to live up to others' notions of me?

How would I know that I'm living well and striving to become my best version of myself?

Is life a series of products purchased or processes processed?

What's the ultimate point of this existence, if not to acquire wealth and position?

Is that erratic, critical, overbearing voice in my head truly my own or … someone (or something) else's?

Consider writing down your honest answers to these questions in your journal; then be sure to review your responses after finishing this book and actively beginning to cultivate more personal power.

Simplicity as an Antidote to Mental Illness

Looking back on your way of thinking prior to starting this challenging but rewarding journey of increasing your personal power and integrating more and more parts of your total self, you may be surprised at the changes in your perspective.

You may even come to see your previous responses to the above questions as showing signs of cognitive dissonance or even emotional instability.

Mental illness is an underreported epidemic today as social media addiction and less than optimal mental states quietly go hand in hand. "The bad news is that the obsession with social media is almost certainly producing unhealthy side effects," wrote Damon Zahariades in *Digital Detox.*

"Scientists have discovered that constant exposure to websites like Facebook and Twitter can alter the brain, affecting the ability to process emotions. It can also lead to restlessness, negative self-image, a decline in happiness, and in extreme cases, depression."

Clearly, despite the oft-repeated propaganda sound bite that technology is here to make life easier, the increasing complexity of the modern world isn't doing many people a lot of favors.

Can you envision yourself as someone living simply, modestly, outside the spotlight of your own ego?

Can you imagine creating enough time and space in your daily existence to take the deep dive of the Hero's Journey beyond your everyday consciousness into the subconscious and unconscious waters of your own corner of the Dark Sea of Awareness?

If so, how does what you see in your mind's eye make you feel?

"I am convinced," wrote Thoreau, "both by faith and experience, that to maintain one's self on this earth is not a hardship but a pastime, if we will live simply and wisely."

Instead, so many of us run the rat race, spin on the hamster wheel, jog on the treadmill, stumble lost through the bewildering funhouse of this clown show of a world. Compared to a life lived with deliberate simplicity, how "successful" does that sound?

Just because your chains are only in your mind doesn't make them less binding. "Free your mind" is more than a proverbial movie line; it's urgent advice to those shackled to complexity here in the Matrix.

If we opt, over and over, to surrender our valuable energy and time to people and things that hold no real value and, worse, separate us from the people and things that do, the joke's on us and we have only ourselves to blame.

Time exists … until it doesn't. Here today, gone tomorrow.

What will you say when the Grim Reaper suddenly appears and asks, "What do you have to show for your life?"

In a world of many time-consuming pursuits, most utterly inane and many major drags on our creative potential, if your answer is "Not much," it's at least worth considering that you've spent your time wisely.

CHAPTER THREE

How to Get Your Groove Back & Enjoy Life Again

"What goes around may come around, but it never ends up exactly the same place, you ever notice? Like a record on a turntable, all it takes is one groove's difference and the universe can be on into a whole 'nother song."
—*Thomas Pynchon*

The Matrix Control System

"In many shamanic societies," to quote Gabrielle Roth, "if you came to a medicine person complaining of being disheartened, dispirited, or depressed, they would ask one of four questions: When did you stop dancing? When did you stop singing? When did you stop being enchanted by stories? When did you find comfort in the sweet territory of silence?"

Most assuredly, it goes almost without saying, a medicine person would never, *ever* ask a suffering individual these four questions:

"How's your 401(k) doing?"

"Did you pay all your taxes this year?"

"Have you accepted Jesus Christ as your Lord and Savior?"

"Did you get the jab for that?"

Many, yours truly included, feel that not just a smattering of individuals but practically the whole population shows signs of being "disheartened, dispirited, or depressed." At the risk of beating a dead drum, it's safe to say that most people, to once again use Thoreau's parlance, "lead lives of quiet desperation."

This sorry state of affairs is, in my humble opinion, absolutely *on purpose*.

Referencing the vast "inorganic" intelligence engaged in energy-harvesting those plugged into this highly scripted Matrix via, for example, the same divide-and-conquer strategies run by the corporate and alternative media for decades, John Kreiter explains that "relative balance is a … conscious farming technique, incorporated in order to keep everything and everyone just slightly off-kilter."

Having us lose ourselves in asinine arguments, activities, careers, etc., designed to disconnect us from our deeper spiritual nature and purpose promotes the creation of powerful emotions connected to our thoughts and beliefs. In turn, our own externally elicited emotions help shape and direct the controlled chaos of the world.

Think back to our brief discussion of mimetic desire in Chapter 1. Expanding on that little introduction, we might sketch the following flow chart to illustrate how this might work on a more technical level in today's supremely networked global culture:

our own thoughts & emotions based on original beliefs »
individualized attention » creation of an initial world(view) »
mimetic desire implant(s) » somebody or something else's thoughts
& emotions » new beliefs » new thoughts & emotions based in
groupthink » collectively controlled attention » creation of a new
world (order)

The result is that the inorganic intelligence calling the shots in this place uses people's own powerfully creative psyches to generate an energy farm (which we rather cavalierly call the world) to sustain … itself!

Truly, the masses—like thrashing, masochistic puppets controlled from above by emotional strings—are living in a hell of their own largely unconscious making.

Yes, we're verging on a situation that reads a bit like science fiction here. But to many shamans, alchemists and other psychonauts, the admittedly disturbing scenario I'm sketching is really just science *fact*.

Consciousness researcher Tom Montalk addresses the nature of this construct in these explicit terms:

What is the Matrix? School or prison, depending on your chosen perspective. On the one hand, it is a hyperdimensional teaching system accelerating your rate of spiritual evolution by providing you with catalytic experiences in response to your thoughts, emotions, and spiritual composition.

"On the other hand," he continues, "many of these experiences manifest as predatory forces preying upon your weaknesses. Of course, the only way to prevent being manipulated by these forces is to discover, integrate, and transform your weaknesses into strengths, thereby indirectly accomplishing the higher purpose of the Matrix which is to help you transcend it."

Like Kreiter, Montalk grasps the true character of our fake Matrix. Both writers also innerstand the ultimate purpose of this crucible of intensity that in *The World Cult & You* I called the Gameboard: to push us to transmute ourselves from the absurd lead of rationality into the profound gold of "magicality" when alchemically exposed to the refiner's fire.

That refiner, in my analogy, is the Dragon, the guardian of the entrance to the cave of our shadow, that I mentioned earlier while sharing some preparatory thoughts on the Hero's Journey.

The Dragon doesn't sleep. It doesn't need to because humanity provides it with a limitless source of energy. The creature's lidless eye, like Sauron's, is forever fixed on us, controlling (indeed, mimetically programming us with) our every thought, emotion, and belief—that is, until we awaken ourselves from its spell by going *inward* on our way *out* of here.

I'll have much more to say about the Dragon a bit later, including what it really is, why it's here, and exactly how it does what it does. But for present purposes, Montalk does an excellent job of setting the stage.

Addressing what I'm calling the Dragon as a plurality (which, as a Borg-like collective mind, it certainly is), he writes that these "predatory forces … have their own agenda, which is to expand their power base and sustain themselves by feeding upon humanity's emotional energies as well as keeping anyone from becoming aware enough to add destabilizing influences to the spiritual prison/farm they are running here on Earth."

If Montalk's eloquent sermonette weren't enough already, here's the kicker: "The sum total of their hyperdimensional manipulation system may be termed the 'Matrix Control System.' It is a school of hard knocks that weakens the spiritually weak and strengthens the spiritually strong, in accordance with their choice to be victims or warriors."

Sing & Dance

In contemplating the sobering ramifications of the foregoing section, I'm reminded of an inspired line by Samuel Beckett, playwright of *Waiting for Godot*, who once quipped, "When you are up to your neck in shit, all you can do is sing."

Accordingly, this chapter is about the necessity (for spiritual warriors if not worldly victims) of singing our own song—and dancing our own dance—despite all the Matrix control mechanisms implemented by the Dragon and its minions designed to have us sing and dance a bunch of life-wasting bullshit.

Could it really be the case that so many of our problems proliferate because this mesmerizing construct and its somnambulistic denizens have forgotten how to dance? how to sing? how to engage storytelling? how to enter into silence?

"We should consider every day lost on which we have not danced at least once," wrote the great German philosopher Friedrich Nietzsche.

Martha Graham, the splendid choreographer who remade modern dance in her own image, saw through the surface into the deeper meaning of movement: "Dance is the hidden language of the soul."

"There is a vitality, a life force, an energy, a quickening that is translated through you into action," she also said, "and because there is only one of you in all time, this expression is unique. And if you block it, it will never exist through any other medium and will be lost."

Has the world, and not just its people, lost its soul through immobility, laziness, and living a zombified half-life doomscrolling through virtual reality? Is our own "intelligence" becoming more and more artificial as we literally ossify in front of our screens?

If you're having trouble answering such questions, maybe you should ask Siri.

For most of the population these days, the only thing that ever dances is a pair of thumbs texting. No wonder people are aging so fast on the Ship of Fools sailing *Titanic*-like through today into no tomorrow.

As people's souls shrink through lack of movement, their connective tissue hardens and their bones turn brittle. This isn't metaphoric. This is the mind-body-spirit connection on full display, for anyone who cares to contemplate its cause and effects, in real time.

Martha Graham again: "All that is important is this one moment in movement. Make the moment important, vital, and worth living. Do not let it slip away unnoticed and unused."

This is living in the present, as opposed to dying in it, as our culture that simultaneously fears and denies death would have us all do in a myriad of sneaky ways.

Overcoming Fear & Learning to Live (Again) …

It's a cliché that public speaking is the greatest private fear, but what if this is dead wrong? What if public *dancing*—and by extension, being willing to dance courageously through life—is our greatest secret fear?

"You look ridiculous if you dance," said Gertrude Stein. "You look ridiculous if you don't dance. So you might as well dance."

Not that I'd ever care to see Gertrude Stein dancing, but she raises an important (if usually downplayed) point. In an era where so many are intent on retreating into their heads, dance remains a vital link—one worth revitalizing even if it means looking stupid—connecting us to the heart of our physicality.

In an extraordinary phenomenon of a book, *The Courage to Be Disliked*, Japanese authors Ichiro Kishimi and Fumitake Koga have gone against the grain of today's groupthink narcissism by giving millions of readers permission to ignore the Dragon's minions' control weapons of judging, guilting, and shaming.

"Your life is not something that someone gives you," they write in this provocative modern-day Socratic dialogue, "but something you choose yourself, and you are the one who decides how you live."

Always bear in mind that the only person whose judgement matters is yourself. If you can learn to transform self-judgment into good judgment, a.k.a. wise circumspection, you've clearly shaken off some of the Dragon's spell and already have one foot halfway out the door of this construct.

As for dancing itself, to cite Paulo Coelho, author of the international sensation about self-discovery through following one's dreams, *The Alchemist*, it "transforms everything, demands everything, and judges no one."

"The philosopher's soul dwells in his head, the poet's soul is in his heart," wrote Kahlil Gibran, adding that "the singer's soul lingers about his throat, but the soul of the dancer abides in all her body."

To be or not to be? Is that really the question? Or should it be: *To dance or not to dance*?

Dancing is being in this quantum disco we call reality. So what does that make not dancing?

Renowned spiritual author Hermann Hesse beautifully remarked this about the transcendent immanence of dancing: "The sacred sense of beyond, of timelessness, of a world which had an eternal value and the substance of which was divine had been given back to me today by this friend of mine who taught me dancing."

Step Out of Your Comfort Zone

So how do we get our groove back when we've so obviously lost it, often individually and always collectively?

"The groove is so mysterious," wrote Lynda Barry. "We're born with it and we lose it and the world seems to split apart before our eyes into stupid and cool. When we get it back, the world unifies around us, and both stupid and cool fall away."

It seems simple enough to say, but perhaps a little harder to do. Harder, but well worth it in the end.

Be willing to put in some sweat equity into a future worth living by moving your ass around. Your mind and heart will surely follow.

The next thing you know you'll be on your own Hero's Journey, zipping past the Dragon into the cave of your shadow and—at some point—out, out into the infinitude of the Dark Sea of Awareness.

Or to put it another way …

If you want your physical, mental, emotional and eventually spiritual circumstances to transform completely, perhaps even beyond your wildest dreams, be willing to step out of your comfort zone onto the dance floor of your own mindfully chosen life.

CHAPTER FOUR

Speak Powerfully with Silence

"Never miss a good chance to shut up." —*Will Rogers*

Conflict Resolution

We often view communication as the cornerstone of human connection. Words bridge people, express emotions, resolve disputes. And now, with the rise of AI and its ballooning large language models, we're seeing word-based connectivity extend into the furthest reaches of the Matrix.

Even so, there exists—and will always exist—a realm where words lose their effectiveness, where silence is sovereign.

This expansive realm extends into the deep-water quietude of the Dark Sea of Awareness. But closer to home, it includes the eminently pragmatic domain of personal boundaries and conflict resolution.

Reason tells us that we should always be able to work things out with words. But the absurdly profound truth is that in many crucial moments of conflict, when sanity and safety hang in the balance, choosing *not* to engage verbally can be by far the most powerful form of speech.

Consider that the Dragon, the hive-mind overlord forever whispering self-destructive notions in your ear to extract more of your energy for food, usually *wants* you to keep talking. The very *last* thing it needs is for you to shut up when your dander is up and you're on the verge of opening your mouth and inserting your foot.

Shamans and energetic alchemists maintain that inner silence can be a sign of the Dragon losing its grip on your mind. Outer silence, especially when called for in challenging circumstances, can be a sign that you're starting to experience inner quietude.

As you discard things that deplete your energy and begin engaging in activities and processes that increase your personal power, pay attention to any and all such moments when your mind is quiet yet you're completely functional. These indicate that what you're doing is *working*, so by all means stick with it!

Silence is certainly the oldest and arguably the purest form of speech. "Silence," in the matchless phrasing of the great Persian poet Rumi, "is the language of God; all else is poor translation."

Silence can be unsettling and disarming, though. We're conditioned to fill the void lest we panic at the thought of our own emptiness. We're encouraged to express our every thought and feeling in absurdly manic ways, yet there's a profound strength in calm, cool and collected verbal restraint.

Sol Luckman

When we resist the urge to respond impulsively, and plant ourselves in our center as opposed to grasping at straws outside ourselves, we tap into a wellspring of inner fortitude.

Such mindful silence allows us to detach from the heat of the moment and respond with clarity rather than reactivity. Choosing silence more and more, we lose less and less energy to "dumb shit," as I like to say, while intelligently reclaiming our power faster and faster.

On numerous occasions I've practiced shamanic and alchemical techniques that allowed me to become lucid in difficult and even traumatic situations where my vital force was spewing out of me and I was able to reverse the flow in real time back into my body.

By paying close attention, you can *sense* energy loss when it's happening even if you're still working on the ability to see it.

Think back to one of the more heated arguments in your life and remember how you felt completely drained after calming down. The phrase "emotionally wrecked" comes to mind when I recall some of the unhinged arguments I had as a younger man.

Well, in the middle of a conflict, it's possible to find silence and begin breathing or otherwise pulling back in the power that has been drained from you. When you do this, often the argument simply stops in its tracks or immediately starts to run out of steam.

This occurs because the energy that was partially responsible for fueling the conflict—yours—is taken out of the equation. Sometimes the other party or parties involved also seem to benefit. Last but not least, consider that you're simultaneously depriving the Dragon of some of its nutrient supply!

How to consciously feed on the Dragon's energy, and not the other way around, is a topic for later discussion that gives a new and improved meaning to "Dragon food." If this topic piques your interest, be sure to make your way to Chapters 15 and 16 for an introduction to recapitulation and energy absorption, respectively.

You'll also get a lot out of Chapter 17, where I explore the Fragmentary Body and a simple technique you can use to seal this largest of holes in your bioenergy field where much of your energy loss occurs.

Outside-the-box techniques aside, we can simply—as a matter of principle and power preservation—refuse to participate in unproductive arguments or engage in conversations that diminish our sense of self-worth.

Grasp that silence in this context isn't about passive aggression or suppressing our voice; it's about recognizing when our energy is better spent elsewhere … or not spent at all.

Personal Boundaries

In its purest form, silence isn't empty space, a void to avoid. Rather, it's a canvas pregnant with possibilities upon which we can paint our intentions and dreams.

Think of silence as a statement of self-respect, a declaration of our boundaries, and a powerful tool for navigating the complexities of human interaction. Simply put, personal boundaries are essential for our emotional wellbeing and overall mental health.

Boundaries define where "we" end and "they" begin, protecting our identity and preventing us from being overwhelmed by the imperatives of others. Properly utilized, silence can be an extraordinarily effective method for establishing and maintaining such boundaries.

Imagine being bombarded with random requests or pressured into situations that make you uncomfortable. A direct confrontation might escalate the scenario beyond hope of recall, whereas agreeing out of obligation leaves you smoldering with resentment and perhaps even shame.

Silence, however, offers a third option, a way to disengage without drama, regret, or guilt. By categorically refusing to engage in conversations that violate our boundaries, we send a clear message louder than words that we're *not* okay with a particular situation or dynamic. This strategy, let it be noted, can be utilized both offline and on.

Our silence might be met with resistance initially, but consistent nonaggressive clamming up speaks volumes efficiently and effectively. Thus we demonstrate self-respect and a willingness to walk away from situations that compromise our inner peace.

Silence can also be a form of pragmatic self-preservation. In the face of anger or aggression, our survival instinct usually urges us to fight back. This type of last-resort reaction, however, typically only exacerbates conflict and ends up creating more harm than good.

Instead, choosing not to engage (and if necessary, leave the scene) allows us to stay centered, preventing things from escalating. Former French president Charles de Gaulle said it best: "Silence is the ultimate weapon of power."

Used skillfully, silence becomes a shield against negativity and manipulation. Silence can allow us to navigate potentially compromising interactions with aplomb and maintain our equilibrium in the face of external pressures.

Conflicts are, of course, an inevitable part of life. When dissension arises and testosterone runs high, our instinctual response is to defend our point of view by proving the other party wrong. But as with fighting back unnecessarily, this stubborn approach rarely leads to resolution and often fans the flames of conflict.

Get Your *Woo* Out of Your *Way*

True personal mastery is expressed in self-control and not reacting. Imagine being caught in a heated argument. Accusations are flying like arrows, battle cries are raised, and bloodlust is soaring.

In the heat of the moment, the temptation to fire back with equal force is visceral, palpable. But what if suddenly and unexpectedly you chose to do … absolutely nothing?

What if you simply listened, observed, and—as if watching a movie that didn't particularly interest you—refused to engage in the drama?

Nonreaction isn't about ignoring the problem or suppressing your emotions, but about choosing a more skillful and, dare I say, more eloquent response.

It's about recognizing that your silence can be more disarming than any logical (or illogical) argument. By refusing to engage in a back-and-forth that's generating a lot more heat than light, you create space for the other person to calm down and for the situation to de-escalate.

This approach requires a high degree of emotional intelligence and maturity. It demands that we step outside the reactive mind imposed by the Dragon and observe the situation with detachment. It requires, above all else, that we *slow down*.

This isn't always easy, but the rewards can be immense. In the words of Sharon Salzberg, "Restore your attention or bring it to a new level by dramatically slowing down whatever you're doing."

By mastering the slow art of nonreaction, we transform conflict into an opportunity for maturation. We learn to regulate our emotions, communicate far more effectively, and build stronger, more harmonious relationships.

The venerated Eastern philosophy of Taoism offers an absurdly profound concept that resonates deeply with the power of silence: *wu wei*, variously translated as "effortless effort," "effortless action," "inaction," and "non-doing."

Wu wei is about aligning ourselves with the natural flow of life, letting go of control, and allowing things to unfold organically. To the extent that we're usually our own worst enemy, *wu wei* is definitely about getting out of our own way.

In the context of conflict resolution, *wu wei* encourages us to approach disagreements with a sense of controlled (but not controlling) detachment. Instead of imposing our will or trying to micromanage the outcome, we learn to flow with the present moment and allow the situation to resolve itself naturally.

This doesn't mean being passive or indifferent. The practice of *wu wei*—which can be greatly facilitated through the study of tai chi, qigong, and even Toltec shamanism's equivalent, Magical Passes—is about finding a delicate balance between action and inaction. We speak our truth when necessary, but we also recognize when silence is the more prudent and persuasive course of action.

Wu wei teaches that genuine strength lies not in forcing our way through life like the proverbial bull in the china shop, but in moving with the current, adapting to changing circumstances, and finding peace even when surrounded by swirling eddies of chaos. As such it's a powerful reminder that sometimes the most effective action is … none at all.

By embracing the principles of *wu wei*, we tap into a deeper wisdom that guides us toward harmonious solutions. We learn to trust the natural layout of the situation and find peace in the now, regardless of the challenges we face.

If you want to have a bit of lighthearted fun with this oftentimes new-agey concept, and avoid taking it too seriously in its own rather playful spirit, imagine your "woo" simply getting out of your "way."

Then, taking deep breaths as your usually domineering thoughts suddenly stop racing past inside your surrogate mind, embrace your silence and observe quietly as your circumstances change for the better.

CHAPTER FIVE

The Hidden Battle for Your Godlike Attention

"There is nothing as powerful, as capable of transforming itself and the planet, as the human imagination ... The tools are there; the path is known; you simply have to turn your back on a culture that has gone sterile and dead, and get with the programme of a living world and a re-empowerment of the imagination." —Terence McKenna

Attention as a Prized Commodity

Our attention, the focalization of our own imaginative capacity, is a precious natural resource. From the standpoint of energy cultivation and manipulation, which encompasses both inner alchemy and many types of shamanism, attention is the most valuable commodity there is.

Consider the telling expression *"pay* attention." Attention, as I see it, is the original currency. If you look closely enough at this divine sense with your sixth sense, you can actually *see* its powerful *current* flowing. And let it be noted that you almost always end up *seeing* whatever you're *currently* paying for.

Attention is what harnesses the primal creative power of our thoughts, emotions and beliefs (which, to oversimplify, combine to form our imagination) in such a way as to build tulpas and egregores, to make dreams come true, and even to create brave new worlds and realities.

In his fascinating exposé of real alchemy, John Kreiter defines attention as the

> conscious and deliberate ... focus of awareness. It is the ability to deliberately direct the consciousness in one particular direction. Doing so naturally pools energy into the thing that the attention is focused on, and allows that aligned self to begin to resonate more and more with the object of attention.

The upshot of Kreiter's position is like a pithy mainline of absolute truth: "Attention is the stuff that makes worlds."

Unfortunately, it must be pointed out, our stolen attention is also the ultimate tool of the Dragon. The predatory designer of this construct co-opts our godlike creative ability by having people tithe (pay) their attention outward and upward to the enormous reptile perched atop the capstone of the World Cult.

Through mental manipulation via mimetic implants on a mass scale that allows it to amass the energy of *our* attention for its own selfish purposes, the Dragon not only plays the role of the Architect in *The Matrix* franchise.

Simultaneously, it also intentionally weakens its human herd (its world builders) to such an extent that humanity has allowed itself to be corralled like farm animals on this prison planet.

The fight for freedom, relatively and ultimately speaking, begins and ends with our attention: where we place it and how we use it.

I'll have a lot more to say on this topic in the next chapter, but for now innerstand that attention is what refines the raw resource of our concepts and feelings into rocket fuel. And as with any fuel, wars are fought over it.

Where we direct our attentive focus shapes and informs—literally and materially—our experienced reality. Prolonged attention creates greater intensity. Like a magnifying glass intensifying the sun's rays, our attention amplifies whatever it focuses on.

If we're to be responsible creators of our experience, as opposed to haphazard victims of it, it's incumbent on us to … *attentively* choose our path through the Matrix with utmost … *attention* to detail.

Technotranshumanism & Prometheus's Fire

In today's mesmerizing digital landscape, our attention is madly sought after. Algorithms are ingeniously designed to keep us hooked like addicts by feeding us mainlines tailored to hold us captive—in mind and perhaps eventually even in body.

If you're sensitive to the flow of energy and semantics, you can unambiguously feel the Dragon at work in all things internet, blockchain, and AI.

Quite literally, like a control freak of leviathan proportions, the Dragon is casting a "net" over humanity to keep our minds "chained" to the "block" as our "intelligence" becomes more and more "artificial," or not our own.

Even though I sometimes jokingly refer to myself as a Luddite in reference to the English workers who tried to sabotage the industrial revolution, and have made the conscious choice not to own a cell phone lo these many years, I wish to be clear that I'm *not* advocating a return to so-called primitivism or a knee-jerk abandonment of technology.

According to numerous schools of shamanic thought, each era has its own energy signature (the "*tonal* of the times") that we must align with to be fully *in* it and effective in whatever role(s) we choose to play.

But this doesn't mean we have to be totally *of* our era. We can—and ought to, for our own benefit at least—think above, outside and beyond it.

Based on its clear energetic signature as new technologies are breathlessly rolled out following a blatantly prewritten script, the current era might best be described as that of "Technotranshumanism."

To think that we can or should all "go Amish" and stick our heads in the sand with regard to technology is wishful thinking, but so too is the black-pilled fantasy that we can't and shouldn't use technology in our own projects and creations.

In the end technology is just a contemporary iteration of Prometheus's fire. It can burn, yes, and its smoke can blind our eyes.

But it can also revolutionize our creativity and aid those of us employing it for higher than material purposes to shine a light through the shadows for anyone capable of seeing and following our freedom beacon.

To have a knee-jerk reaction to technology is to think like a victim. This is how the Dragon wants you to think—in all ways at all times. Its entire control apparatus is predicated on your tacit or explicit acceptance of victim mentality.

I'd argue that this even applies to the world's predatory class, the so-called elites, those puffed-up minions who, while they may get a rush out of preying on others, must on some level suspect they themselves are ultimately just Dragon food.

But *we*, not technology, and not even the Dragon, are the real creators here. The Dragon knows this. That's why it uses us to build its world *for* it, since apparently it can't do so on its own—and it's high time we figured this out for ourselves.

My advice is to feel free to play in the Matrix by using technology basically however you see fit to bring your ideas to life for the benefit of yourself and, with any luck, others. The only guideline, if I may suggest one, would be as in the Hippocratic oath: "First, do no harm."

The Ultimate Tool for Social Engineering

Having embraced the positive possibilities of tech, let's not ignore the downsides. Social media, for example, has quite simply been weaponized for social engineering, or mind-controlling the masses. As Jim Morrison keenly observed well before the advent of the internet, "Whoever controls the media, controls the mind."

Remember those depressing dystopian novels your English teachers had to goad you to read? You know, the ones with Big Brother noting your every action, or everyone turned into zombified consumers?

It turns out Orwell and Huxley might have been onto something. Today, we're living in a world where our screens are constantly flickering with notifications, feeding us a never-ending stream of information, misinformation, and most perniciously, disinformation.

It can't be denied that most people today are voluntarily plugged into the Matrix—except instead of being jacked in and hardwired, they keep mindlessly taking hits on the virtual crack pipe of Instagram, TikTok, Meta, etc.

The most disturbing part of this web junkie scenario is that the overwhelming majority have absolutely no idea to what extent their thoughts and opinions are being mimetically manipulated, day after day, by the technology they take for granted.

In other words, they're clueless as to how much they resemble an insect unaware of the peril as it tiptoes through the tulips around a spider's web.

Obviously, mixing biology metaphors here, I'm talking about the sheeple who fancy they're in control of their information, don't realize they're just pawns in a giant game of social engineering, and would dismiss you as a "conspiracy theorist" without a single independent thought if you suggested they were being turned into food for something else's dinner.

But even if we ignore the Dragon's energy harvesting through cultivation of varying levels of mental illness in its human herd, we can safely say there's a complex web of tech companies, advertisers and governments all trying, spider-like, to trap our attention for a variety of reasons — most of which probably aren't in our best interests.

Tech companies want to keep us super-glued to our screens at all costs, advertisers want to sell us stuff we don't need, and governments … Well, let's just say that these artificial entities explicitly designed to govern the *mente* (mind) aren't exactly hiding (except in plain sight) their primary agenda.

A major problem is that there's precious little transparency about how tech platforms actually work behind the scenes. If you disagree, please explain in detail the Spotify algorithm (to cite but one example) used to spoon out practically the entire world's music feeds.

We're rarely if ever told precisely how most of these algos are designed, exactly what data they collect, or how our information might be weaponized against us. For anyone who cares to contemplate the situation, that's a *big* issue because it shows we have no way of knowing how or to what extent we're being puppeteered.

Stop Raging against the Machine

The Matrix can feel like a pretty hopeless place. I get that. Nobody in his or her right mind (a tiny minority, admittedly) wants to be caught in an endless digital labyrinth like a techno lab rat.

My position is that, on at least a subliminal level, even many of the most benighted sheeple (the really stubborn ones I think of as the "consciously clueless") secretly suspect that they're corralled in a system designed to control them, to keep them in check.

But I'm here to tell you it doesn't *have* to be this way. We have the power to change our circumstances individually and maybe, just maybe, collectively.

Forget rage, we don't even have to "fight back" against the machine. But we do have to perform one, all-important mind maneuver:

We must reclaim our attention and consciously choose a new way to focus it that is both self-directed and empowering.

By intentionally shifting the position of our experienced reality's "assemblage point," to use a term popularized by Carlos Castaneda, we have the ability to enter a new reality experience—if not always with the snap of our fingers, then certainly with applied effort. This change depends on internal *wu wei* as opposed to a process of external struggle.

This book is designed to help you get to this new version of the world. There are other helpful resources as well, and I'll be introducing some of those in due course. So please keep your chin up, even in the face of the great obstacles I've been outlining, as you continue reading and processing.

I'm all for awareness, critical thinking, even healthy doses of skepticism. But in the end, I don't feel that the "information war" is a battle worth fighting because it simply can't be won.

The Dragon can't be defeated on its own turf (the Matrix) using its own "operating system" (the installed one we think of as our minds). As powerful as he was, not even Neo could defeat the Architect when he finally "met his maker." Heck, he couldn't even overpower his shadow, Agent Smith, until he wised up and simply *stopped fighting*.

As always, *the only way out is in*. Withdrawal from the system is a powerful mode of nonviolent resistance, and one never more effective than when done using conscious reclamation and cultivation of our own energy.

However we choose to proceed, the first step is to acknowledge the problem, to see it for what it is. We need to recognize that social media is far more than just a harmless distraction or handy tool.

Rather, it has been brilliantly architected as a comprehensive net or web for the mind that can be used to alter our thoughts and behaviors, and from there redirect the creative focus of our attention, usually without our even realizing it.

Hunter S. Thompson, the gonzo journalist extraordinaire, once said, "When the going gets weird, the weird turn pro." Even though it may be a little dated, that's rock-solid advice for navigating our present Technotranshumanist age, where things are getting weirder by the second.

In a world saturated with freakish information and algorithmic wackiness, we need to get a little weird ourselves to survive … and, if we play our cards right, thrive.

To do so we must summon the courage of our inner hero to question everything, to think for ourselves, to look for answers outside the box, to resist the urge to conform to the digital hive mind.

So, turn off notifications for a day, log out for a while, go for a walk in the real world, mindfully appreciate the taste of your coffee for a change, unplug.

Read a book, people-watch, have a face-to-face conversation with an actual human being, and remember that there's much more to life than likes and followers, selfies and influencers, thank goodness.

For the Love of All You Hold Dear, Stop Doomscrolling!

Today's constant online barrage can leave us feeling drained and unfulfilled. As mentioned, social media addiction has been linked to depression. It's high time to reclaim our attention, break free from the chains of digital distraction, and rediscover the immense creative power of our own minds … for our own benefit.

This reclamation project begins with awareness, self-awareness, inner gnosis in a tsunami of insanity. Recognize that your attention is the most valuable thing you can ever own, and you alone have the ultimate power to choose where to direct it.

Not all tugs on our attention are benign—far from it on today's digitized High Seas. It should be obvious, even to those skeptical of most conspiracy theories, that there are individuals and entities "from the Deep" who seek to manipulate our focus for their gain.

They exploit our fears, insecurities and desires, bombarding us with negativity and hopelessness, and rarely, if ever, looking on the bright side. Coincidence? I think not.

These tactics prey on our natural negativity bias, our self-preservation instinct, our traumas, our insecurities. The human brain is wired to pay more attention to threats and negative stimuli than most other inputs. This is understandable in a predatory environment.

Such an approach might have kept us safe in our evolutionary past. But in today's groupthinking, fearmongering culture, it can lead us down rabbit holes inside rabbit holes of anxiety and despair.

Be wary of information sources that consistently evoke fear, anger, or outrage. Be cautious also of ones that yo-yo followers between such negative states and positive ones, only to repeat this whipsaw cycle again and again.

Question the motives behind the messages you consume. I'm sorry to say it, but there's a good chance you'll find hidden agendas almost everywhere that don't support you or humanity.

Ask yourself whether the messages directed your way are designed to empower you or keep you trapped in a vicious cycle of always seeing the glass as half full.

Prolonged exposure to negativity takes a toll on mental and emotional wellbeing. Doomscrolling—the act of endlessly scrolling through negative news and social media feeds—can leave one feeling helpless, anxious, depressed, and even suicidal.

Moreover, this negativity bias can create a self-fulfilling prophecy by tipping the first domino in a chain of interrelated events in a sort of tragic butterfly effect. Simply put, when we focus on the negative, we're far more likely to notice and experience more negativity in our lives.

This can give way to a downward spiral where our thoughts and emotions become increasingly self-defeating. And almost inevitably, this manifests as more disturbing life events.

While I'm all for being emotionally honest with yourself and not running away from your shadow aspects, this quote by Peace Pilgrim certainly offers food for contemplation: "If you realized how powerful your thoughts are, you would never think a negative thought."

I encourage you to be brave enough to break free from the clutches of doomscrolling. Limit your exposure to negative news and social media. Take a break from the online noise. Try a "truther" detox, as I propose in Chapter 7.

Instead of letting your attention be misdirected, seek out uplifting and inspiring content that nourishes your mind and spirit. Just as a negative focus can drag us down, a positive one has the power to lift us up.

When we choose to emphasize gratitude, love, joy and various other types of empowering wavelengths, we create an upward spiral of positive emotions and experiences.

Research has shown that simply giving thanks for life's mundane blessings, for example, can lead to increased happiness, improved relationships, and better physical health.

Choosing to pay particular attention to positive emotions such as love and compassion can even boost our immune systems and make us more resilient to most types of stress. Being upbeat can self-induce a range of epigenetic changes, switching off "bad" genes and turning on "good" ones.

Cultivate a practice of gratitude. Take time each day to appreciate your blessings, no matter how insignificant they might seem. Surround yourself with positive people and engage in activities that bring you joy.

Put down your smartphone, smell the roses, and—as Gandalf instructs King Théoden when the latter emerges from Wormtongue's hypnotic spell in Peter Jackson's adaptation of Tolkien—"breathe the free air again, my friend."

Our beliefs and thoughts coalesce into a kind of virtual omnipotence that's literally divine in its creational ability, allowing it to bring different versions of reality into existence. Think of focusing your attention as a way of consciously choosing your own best timeline.

One More Time for the Cheap Seats

This point is so important it bears repeating …

When we focus on positive thoughts, we attract positive experiences into our field of awareness. Conversely, when we dwell on negativity, we invite more negativity into our experience.

This isn't to say we should ignore challenges or pretend everything's hunky-dory when it obviously isn't. Don't be an ostrich and bury your head in the sand when shit's hitting the fan.

Rather, the idea is to choose to approach life—even its trying moments—with an upbeat and proactive mindset, believing in our ability to overcome obstacles and create a better future … at least for ourselves.

Every thought we think is like a brush stroke on the canvas of our lives. Let's choose our thoughts, then, as a great artist painting a masterpiece of joy, love, success, and fulfillment.

We're at a crossroads in human history. The digital age has unearthed unprecedented access to information and connection, but it has also unleashed a torrent of negativity and manipulation.

The responsibility lies with each of us to become conscious stewards of our own minds. Our challenge (and a challenging one it is!) is to cultivate discernment in the information we consume minute by minute, hour by hour, day by day.

If our desire is to enjoy and perhaps eventually transcend the Matrix, we must select with great circumspection the thoughts we wish to energize and direct our focus only toward that which invigorates and empowers us. Anything else simply isn't … worth your attention.

CHAPTER SIX

The Trouble with "Truthing"

"The Belief System was put inside you like a program by the outside Dream. The Toltecs call this program the Parasite. The human mind is sick because it has a Parasite that steals its vital energy and robs it of joy. The Parasite is all those beliefs that make you suffer." —Miguel Ruiz

Is Your *Loosh* on the Loose?

In *The World Cult & You* I explored an extremely controversial, hot-button topic that triggered a lot of readers: the "radical" idea that "truthers" and "truthing" might be dangerous and that trauma bonding relative to doomsday scenarios might be a symptom of collective mental illness and cultish adherence to groupthink.

After publication of my book, which contains a number of playfully challenging memes addressing different aspects of this decidedly unhealthy scenario, I created another that read: "Stop helping doomsday cults bring about doomsday using *your* energy!"

One way to grasp what's going on in this bizarrely self-defeating situation is to examine the Matrix and its overlord, the Dragon, through the lens of the human energy sometimes referred to as *loosh*.

Loosh is, in a word, Dragon food. We might think of *loosh* as the form of human energy consciousness adopts as it slides toward being *un*conscious through traumatization and other negative forms of behavioral engineering.

As I've been arguing, the conscious energy of attention can be used to do literally anything because it's a focalization of the imagination, the binding life force that amalgamates thoughts, emotions and beliefs into a powerfully creative gestalt.

You could also call this force chi, prana, kundalini, torsion energy, scalar waves, even mojo. These are all merely variations on the central theme of all Matrix energy dynamics: people power.

Imagination can be concentrated by attention to build positive outcomes—harmonious structures, communities, technologies, even worlds—but it can just as easily be harnessed to create hell on earth.

Where power is concerned, there's no judgement, no duality, no left and right, no yin and yang, no "good" vs. "evil."

Universally speaking, all that matters is *power*, pure and simple. This is why in world mythology the seemingly antithetical archetypes of creation and destruction are often wedded in the same god or goddess.

Currently, we find ourselves losing ourselves in a weird feedback loop in this simulated dreamscape of a worldwide civilization managed by the Dragon that keeps rerouting human energy to create less than desirable outcomes for everybody ... except the Dragon.

In this debilitating scenario, doomsday cults of all kinds are allowed to thrive online and off because they serve our spiritual adversary's trauma-based mind control agenda.

It doesn't matter whether we're talking bona fide doomsday cults identifying as such or camouflaged "truther" cults masquerading as YouTube channels. All such gaslighting organizations are used by the Dragon to bend the spoon of reality in a doomsday direction here in this *loosh*-siphoning Matrix.

When you give doomsday or other fearmongering cults your attention, just your attention, simply by listening to their words, and certainly by subscribing to them, sending them likes, shares, follows and even money, you're offering up your precious power in promotion of Doomsday.

Don't shoot me, I'm just the messenger.

Again, attention is the faculty of focusing the life force. When you allow your attention to be negatively focused by another mind, whether that of the Dragon or even another person, that mind can create with your personal power (which has now become *loosh*) what it will.

Realize that nothing any of these so-called truthers are saying is inherently true because *there's no there there* to begin with in this construct. It's *all* made up, every bit of it— including anything calling itself "science," that scam of scams in this benighted house of mirrors ruled by the false god of rationality.

It's widely acknowledged by many pundits that we no longer live in an age of news, but of *narrative as news*. But what if this is *old* news? What if things have *always* been this way?

Indeed, I suggest they have. When you invest your attention in a particular line of "truthing," you're choosing to buy into (energetically support or *pay* for with your attention) somebody (or something) else's narrative, simple as that.

We can easily extrapolate this dynamic even to works of literature, movies, shows, music and other forms of mind manipulation on whose altars you offer up the sacred gift of your attention. When you think about it this way, human sacrifice is more prevalent today than ever!

Placebo & Pronoia Power

Our individual attention is exceedingly powerful, no doubt about it. But when our attentions (plural) come together in an aligned group, we're looking at the nuclear option, creative or destructive potential on a monumental scale.

In signing a tacit contract by "attending" to things that don't contain inspiration or optimism, get your mind around the rule of engagement that your energy can and will be used against you by the Dragon and its minions.

I know that certain aspects of my work having to do with the World Cult might be considered "heavy." Still, given my ultimately empowering message of "wholing" and transcendence, I suggest that my writing on this subject constitutes a sort of psychological litmus test separating spiritual warriors from mundane victims.

Warriors can't get enough of my perspective and they've told me so, repeatedly. Victims would rather visit a proctologist than consider the actual nature of the world they inhabit and their role in producing and sustaining it.

Could this be because there are fewer and fewer genuine individuals (again, in the sense of being "individuated") in this period of orchestrated chaos in which tribalism is making a fierce comeback left, right, and center?

Or perhaps informed, measured optimism such as mine is dismissed because it appears to contradict the so-called facts—even though "facts," like weather patterns, can and do suddenly change as the "scientific" narratives that establish "facts" mysteriously mutate.

On this subject consider the *fact* that the speed of light, that universal constant on which the massive edifice of modern physics is largely based, is subject to change.

Several years ago Rupert Sheldrake made this point emphatically in a highly popular TED talk. And do you know what happened to that talk? It was rigorously *attacked* and *censored* by the Dragon's gatekeepers of acceptable discourse.

Or maybe the comparatively sane voices of hope (as opposed to "hopium") are ignored because trauma-based mind control produces addiction to despair in the masses, a kind of Stockholm Syndrome throughout the Matrix.

Whatever the case, the very neologism *hopium* is, in my opinion, just another clever psyop employed by the Dragon's yes-men and -women to detract and distract from the empowering notion that *positivity by itself can change the world.*

Our feelings, thoughts, beliefs and even expectations act as filters through which our imaginations initiate the process of generating our particular experienced reality. These filters influence our interpretation of events, our interactions with others, and even our physical health.

Take, for instance, the well-documented placebo effect. This phenomenon is a ringing testament to the influence of an upbeat focus. When we believe in a positive outcome, our bodies respond accordingly, prompting production of endorphins, pumping up the immune system, and even dulling our perception of pain.

Conversely, the nocebo effect demonstrates the detrimental impact of a negative focus. If we go in expecting side effects from a treatment, for example, we're a lot more likely to experience them — even if the treatment itself is just a sugar pill. This highlights the wisdom of cultivating positive expectations and minimizing negative self-talk.

These effects, it should be noted, aren't limited to medical contexts. They permeate every aspect of our lives. The key takeaway here is that our minds are extraordinary tools for creating desired or feared outcomes.

A related discussion revolves around paranoia and its opposite, pronoia.

Paranoia isn't the only way to manifest consequences (in this case, negative ones) through the focus of attention. Individuals prone to paranoia may interpret impersonal interactions as personally directed attacks, creating a self-fulfilling dynamic of fear and mistrust.

Alternatively, we can consciously opt for *pronoia*: the belief that the universe, multiverse or whatever you wish to call it is conspiring to bless you at all times, appearances notwithstanding.

By operating with pronoia, we invite a number of potential benefits that have the power to radically change our lives for the better—leading to greater happiness, resilience, and fulfillment.

With pronoia we're far more likely to perceive breakdowns as breakthroughs; attract positive relationships under even the most challenging conditions; and experience a sense of flow and synchronicity while others around us might be stuck in a rut.

Just as the placebo and nocebo effects demonstrate the power of positive and negative expectations, respectively, the concepts of pronoia and paranoia offer further insight into the role our perceptions play in crafting our reality.

It's a maxim that where attention goes energy flows. Or as the famous line from *Field of Dreams* phrases it, "If you build it, he will come." Focus on a fairy-tale city on a hill and someday you just might live there. Focus on a dystopia like the one in *Hunger Games* and ...

Your Mind as a Foreign Installation

Sadly, in this upside-down construct, when you broadcast fear and panic at the top of your lungs, the Dragon's algorithms can't get enough of you.

The upshot is that you receive a wildly disproportionate amount of attention—especially considering that your message is, despite any and all "positive" window dressing, antihuman garbage.

Hope panhandles while fear sells like hotcakes. This may lean toward the cliché, but it's just the way things are here in this nowhere ... right now anyway.

A fearful outlook eventually leads to behaviors that are, in the final analysis, self-sabotaging. This is because such behaviors are the intentional results of the Dragon's net or web of mental strategies designed to entrap you and harvest your *loosh*.

The irony, of course, is that we ultimately entrap ourselves and sacrifice our own *loosh*. It's as if there's a universal law even the Dragon can't ignore requiring it to have us agree, on some level, to our own undoing. Enter the ubiquity of contracts and the pervasive idea of social contracts in this construct.

My research into and practice of shamanism and inner alchemy has led me to conclude—logically as well as experientially—that the majority of the population are "downloaded" with the consciousness of the Dragon. This means that most people are using a foreign (read: extraterrestrial) installation as their operating system.

In other words, to reiterate this freakishly literal point, the masses aren't really even thinking with their own minds! Now does their consistently insane behavior make a little more sense?

Technically, you could say that we're really not even up against mind control per se. Instead, we're faced with the far more troubling prospect of *mind ownership* … by an absentee owner.

No wonder Matrix denizens can't see the forest for the trees, can't see the positive, can't acknowledge the potential for transformation that's all around—but more importantly, *inside*—them.

Get Out of the Feedback *Loosh*

But my goal isn't to focus my own powerful attention on the negative, despite the ponderous darkness that's nearly palpable to anyone with a shred of their own consciousness intact.

I propose, in fact, that the incessant fearmongering heaped on us today is ironically a tool implemented at the behest of the Dragon to *wake the flock up.*

Yes, hate on me if you must, but I'm *going there* by suggesting that the Dragon (which I've elsewhere called the Great Parasite) is actually here to teach us about who we are and the world we live in.

When you step back from it, you realize that the whole idea of so many fearful conspiracies proliferating like harmful bacteria everywhere isn't just surreal or overkill, it's *ludicrous.*

This "reality" is so obviously *un*real. It's like bad screenplay writing. No matter how many times you see the same tired script playing out on the world stage, if you can manage to think for yourself just a little, it's simply not believable.

Could this be by design—part of the Dragon's wake-up strategy for humanity?

In *The World Cult & You* I touch on the process of awakening that many seekers like myself have gone through: coming face to face with conspiracies galore after "doing the research" and all that runaround. I explicitly state that I'm *not* advising people to forego exploring their interests, thinking rationally, etc.

I also emphasize that there comes a time, a sort of epiphany like something out of *Through the Looking-Glass*, when you realize that everything you've discovered through your "research" has basically been *fed* to you because you've been *looking* for it!

We're in a complex feedback loop—or for most people, feedback *loosh*—that reveals to us an imaginary "reality" that we choose to buy into … just before it becomes our lived "reality."

So many things are put out to make it seem as if we're helpless victims of this crazy Matrix. This is the purpose of such lopsided half-truths as the popular (and for that reason alone, highly dubious) notion that we're stuck against our will in a "soul trap" or "reincarnation trap" that most people will never escape.

Obviously, such a worldview isn't compatible with, say, a starting point founded on a Christian eschatological perspective with a definitive end date to the status quo. Yet if you keep feeding your new research interest on souls transmigrating ad nauseam into the construct, it will keep giving back to you precisely what you're looking for.

But then, if you become interested in something else and start researching that, suddenly the construct starts feeding back to you new information to support your new viewpoint.

It's like magic. Because it is. Thanks to your magical attention. See how this works?

If you take a moment to compare the first two lines of your research (linear eschatology vs. circular metempsychosis), you'll note that they're utterly incompatible, mutually exclusive.

Yet you've uncovered mountains of "evidence" supporting *both* theories. This is what's happening on a massive, multifaceted scale in today's conspiracy theory community.

The problem is that the entire smorgasbord of conspiracy "evidence" is just fabrications of consciousness. It doesn't *prove* anything—except that attention is really, *really* creative.

The construct is—with a wink and a nod, as it were— clearly just playing your perceptions back to you in endless variations. At some point the only logical conclusion is that *this is all in your mind*.

That's the wake-up moment when you finally slap your forehead and say,

I'm CREATING all this baloney!

And then the all-important follow-up question:

So what do I want to create now that I'm conscious that I'm creating everything?

Be a Solipsist, Not a Narcissist

From the perspective of consciousness expansion, it's actually a service to us to have so much weirdness thrown at us like classic slapstick pies in the face … over and over again.

The weirdness might very well be—it's at least worth considering—part of our own design from some higher aspect of ourselves to wake us up here in the dream of this so-called reality.

When I language my thoughts this way, know that I'm far from inviting you to become a public narcissist like some plastic Law of Attraction guru patting yourself on the back in a selfie for having finally recognized your own divine nature.

Instead, I'm suggesting that you embrace your closet "solipsist."

In this context solipsism is the idea that (to use a well-worn phrase) *there's only one of us here*, a creative consciousness forever experiencing permutations of itself … for whatever reason.

This notion is often ridiculed by "truthers," many of whom simply loathe it with every fearful fiber of their manipulated being. To them good news must be "fake news." That should tell you something.

When you experience the full impact of what I call the "solipsistic awakening," you're not staring at your navel; you're staring into *infinity*. You've got both feet in the Dark Sea of Awareness and are about to take a deep breath and dive right in.

Back here in the Matrix, you've also just been handed a heaping helping of personal accountability. We're talking a "Peter Parker" moment when you realize that with tremendous power comes tremendous responsibility.

Is manifestation always getting exactly what your ego wants? I don't think so. Manifestation is, in my opinion, getting exactly what the wiser part of you knows you need. And then the less wise part of yourself has to deal with the aftereffects.

Such a situation is the direct opposite of narcissism. You do come face to face with the staggering magnitude of what you're capable of, yes. But rather than having your ego inflated at the reflection of your bad self, you experience awe in relation to the totality of what you are and feel deep humility.

In a solipsistic world where there's only one of us here, narcissism and runaway ego simply dissipate because, well, who is there to impress? Who is there to control—except yourself?

Let's include in "yourself" your own responses to the very things you're creating and then having to live with. Such as the Dragon and its crazymaking funhouse, the Matrix.

With that said, once again I emphatically encourage you to choose your life and world wisely.

CHAPTER SEVEN

Try a "Truther" Detox

"DETOX your mind, body, AND your contact list." —*Supa Nova Slom*

The "Reality" Misconception

In a general sense, as I'm using the term, "truther" refers to anyone regularly placing agency (i.e., power) outside individual and collective conscious attention.

In other words, whether they're aware of their error or otherwise, "truthers" falsely insist on affirming a preexisting, arbitrary "reality" outside the purview of our own creatively applied awareness.

My position—one I share with countless mystics, yogis, shamans, alchemists, and other way-outside-the-boxers—is that there's no verifiable "outside" reality, no tangible "home base" in the real.

Instead, there's only a simulacrum or, more accurately perhaps, a simulation-style dreamscape mimicking an actual physical world inside an infinity (the Dark Sea of Awareness) of similarly attention-generated constructs.

The "reality" misconception can take various forms. The two most common are *materialism*, in which a "real world" somehow manages to exist before or without anyone's awareness of it; and *religion*, in which a divine being or force remains in a world miraculously outside … the world.

If you believe such fairy tales, fine, but just don't call them "truth." Maybe opinions based on secondhand "knowledge" would be a more accurate description. Or more straightforwardly, just call them … mimetic implants.

Meanwhile, as Neville Goddard so accurately and beautifully stated, we humans live "in a world that is nothing more or less than [our] consciousness objectified."

My view is that nothing can ultimately be proven beyond a shadow of a doubt—except to oneself via the wisdom, or gnosis, of personal experience—and anything and everything can be easily "debunked" by the cavalier exercise of the fraudulent *dieu du jour*, reason.

Carlos Castaneda famously described humanity's collective perceptual lens, its so-called assemblage point, as being currently stuck in the extremely limiting "place of reason."

The situation is profoundly absurd because while reason is smugly convinced of its rightness, in actuality it's merely one of an infinitude of possible interpretations of the many fictitious "rules" and "laws" that supposedly "govern" this forever malleable construct.

On the subject of the false god of reason, I love the following penetrating passage from John Kreiter. Clearly, he was influenced by Castaneda's perspective, only to go well beyond the latter's purview in many important respects. Read it several times if necessary to let its full implications sink in:

[T]rue logic is not reason, but reason can be said to be a small branch of logic … a type of group-based deductive logical scheme that relies on the mass power of the group in order to impose a perceptive orderliness in human consciousness and therefore the human objective world.

One could think of reason … as being the enforcement arm that helps to bring a certain slant to individual mass consciousness … [T]he evolution of reason throughout human history is really the refinement of a certain type of limited self-awareness and individuality. This individual consciousness is irreversibly linked to mass human consciousness, because the self that we call the individual is in reality … a product of a mass mental movement referred to as reason.

Not to put too fine a point on it … But the *point* is that the lens of reason, by focalizing our commandeered attention in a certain way under the skillful direction of the Dragon, has created this mess of a world we live in.

Isn't that reason enough to distrust reason and begin putting a little more faith in something, anything else—say, intuition?

Reification, or Making Shit Real

In essence, "truthers"—by doggedly searching for the Holy Grail of an external absolute—perpetuate the fatal snafu of separating the Creator from the created.

But as I've proposed, the Creator and the created are one creature: the ouroboros forever consuming and producing itself simultaneously.

In maintaining such a faulty, reason-based mindset, "truthers" do a number of disservices to themselves, their message and their followers here in this subjective construct in which objectivity is merely a myth of overweening "science." (As I once quipped, *Always, always, always put "science" in quotes.*)

A major disservice in this scenario is that "truthing" inevitably leads to disempowerment in which people, lured by the false promise of solutions, are tricked into stepping *outside* themselves again and again for answers to their personal and collective dilemmas—when, as I repeat, *the only way out is in.*

At their most benign (or least malignant), "truthers" are genuine seekers doing the best they can in sharing their "truth."

While they've been led astray by reason and are playing the Pied Piper for others in turn, at least they're not doing this intentionally. Even though their heads may be confused, their hearts are mostly in the right place.

At their worst, "truthers" know *exactly* what they're doing (in my opinion anyway) and are happy to serve as parasitic mind controllers on the payroll of our tutelary spiritual adversary, the Dragon.

In this capacity "truthers" are indistinguishable from cult leaders. Both knowingly extract money and *loosh*, or secondhand vital force, for their own purposes before tithing a significant portion of this stolen attention power up the food chain of the World Cult to the "God" (the Dragon or Great Parasite) who sits atop it.

"Truthers" are experts (conscious or otherwise) at promoting doomsday and other negative and/or limiting outcomes through manufactured consent that works exactly the same way as today's mainstream press that delivers subjectively driven, outcome-generating *narratives* in lieu of objectively reported *news*.

"Reification" is a helpful concept to emphasize here. To "reify," according to *The Cambridge Dictionary*, means "to make something more real or consider it as real."

By using a toolkit of brainwashing tactics for tapping into mimetic desire in order to energize the power of collective belief in … whatever (a "scientific" model, a version of "history," a conspiracy theory, etc.), "truthers" aren't discovering "truth" … *They're just making shit real*.

That, my friends, in a sound bite, is how this world, on personal as well as communal levels, manifests.

Like it or not, we're doomed or blessed—depending on your perspective—to inhabit an eternally looping circuit that involves our thoughts, innermost desires, actions, etc., in telling back to us the story we're telling about our lives—individually and collectively.

"Truthers" Are on the Payroll—That's How They Roll

Regardless of their degree of complicity in creating groupthink via public gaslighting, it must be stressed that a major motivation of both kinds of "truthers" mentioned above was summed up by Upton Sinclair when he said, "It is difficult to get a man to understand something, when his salary depends on him not understanding it!"

Or as I put it in these lyrics to a song called "Doomscrollin'":

Today's doom prophets
Are all about profit
They're on the payroll
That's how they roll

I don't need the right wing
Or the left wing
I'm growin' my own wings
Thank you very much

It doesn't matter what "truther" specialization one has in mind (and there are multitudes to choose from): secret societies, extraterrestrials, hollow earth, Tartaria, mudfloods, plasma apocalypse, rogue planets, or other doomsday clickbaitery full of sound and fury signifying a load of nothing.

Regardless of whether they desire to be of service to humanity, "truthers"—despite any and all metaphysical leanings—by definition succumb to a critical error that makes them part of the problem, not the solution: adherence to something ostensibly *real*, a "real truth" in a manifestly contrived mindscape.

In *The World Cult & You* I was careful to distinguish between "truthers" and other types of consciousness explorers. "Truthers," I said,

> are perilous to those with a questioning nature because they give the false-comfort illusion (one perfectly attuned to this age of disillusionment with religion and even science) of providing answers to the fake reality's mysteries—even though when you examine their track records, they do no such thing.

Note that I'm not talking about most consciousness explorers and reality researchers here. "Truthers" focus on "solutions" in the outside world, while the majority of sincere psychonauts innerstand that there is no outside world and that empowerment in and escape from this crazy construct can only be an inside job.

The best psychonauts, or mappers of consciousness, could care less what appears to be (or not be) happening in the external "reality" (which, by the way, in a way that undermines the real in everyday terms, appears at least somewhat different for everyone).

Instead, devoted psychonauts are concerned with the internally generated dream that gives rise to the illusory dreamscape called reality.

Author Ken Eagle Feather succinctly explains why the mastery of conscious dreaming (as opposed to "fighting the good fight" in the "real world") is of utmost importance for anyone seeking to create his or her experience: "Reality, or at least the perception of it, is an ever-expanding dream."

Psychonauts may *reference* what is taken for reality, as we all must do if we wish to communicate with one another. But they don't seek *answers* there—as they grok that the construct is a funhouse of creative mirrors that merely reflect back to us the "real" that we see in them.

Truly, we're the creators of all that we behold. If you fail to grasp this operational principle, it pretty much doesn't matter how smart or talented a researcher you are. Inevitably, you'll just go in circles while forever convincing yourself and your followers that you're hot on the trail of a major breakthrough.

Ready for a Parasite Cleanse?

A related analogy for conceptualizing how "truthing" functions is that research in the Matrix might be said to merely create rabbit holes that go ever deeper into … the Matrix.

In a mind-bending "aikido" move of its own, the Matrix makes it so that the closer "truthers" and other mundane researchers feel they are to the "truth," the further they technically are from it.

At the risk of stating the obvious, when one has parasites, even mental ones like the Great Parasite and its mouthy minions, the only remedy is to do a parasite cleanse.

This means that for a full week, if you're willing to give it a try in good faith, you'll go cold turkey off fear porn and useless research while focusing solely on *empowering yourself.*

You may suffer withdrawal symptoms. Most "truth" junkies do. Delirium tremens isn't uncommon. But that's okay. You'll start to feel much steadier, lighter and clearer in no time.

Besides, what do you really have to lose … except mental parasites?

Productive Alternatives to Doomscrolling

During and also after your weeklong vacation for the heart and mind, the following eleven activities (listed in no particular order of importance) are healthy alternatives to wasting your precious time and energy materializing someone else's vision of worldwide chaos and destruction.

See what works for you, give it a go, and watch your life change rapidly for the better …

1. Make a video or write a blog post of your own vision of a positive future to energize a different outcome.

2. Honor someone you love with a poem, a portrait or another creative tribute to a meaningful connection in your life.

3. Pick up a new hobby or learn a different sport to change your neurological pathways and open up novel cognitive possibilities beyond today's pervasive fear porn.

4. Move your body with dance, surfing, qigong or whatever else turns you on to shake off the over-the-top doom and gloom and embrace the limitless potential of the present moment.

5. Focus, *really* focus all the creative power of your attention on something incredibly positive you'd love to see happen in your life for five minutes a day until it happens.

6. Repeat the above with something you'd love to witness in the world at large. Shoot, put in ten minutes a day if you can spare the time. Lord knows this world needs all the help it can get.

7. Make it a point to change one judgmental reaction a day to its opposite: nonjudgmental okayness.

8. Find ways to laugh: at genuinely funny things, people, and situations; at your own follies and shortcomings; at the "profound absurdity" of it all. Let laughter empty you of self-importance and fill you back up with creative helium until you're light enough to float.

9. Choose peaceful silence the next time conflict crops up in your life.

10. Share empowering messages with friends and followers to pay your attention forward into a brighter future for all.

11. Choose one day a week to go off socials completely. Use this time to nurture yourself and come up with additional strategies to unplug from a society self-destructively addicted to doomscrolling.

CHAPTER EIGHT

How to Navigate the Online Noise in the Long Run

"I've spent the morning googling digital detoxes." —Nick Spalding

Upping the Ante on Your Doom Fast

If you've decided to do a "truther" detox, as suggested in the previous chapter, you might consider going even further during your weeklong doom fast by getting off social media altogether.

I realize going completely cold turkey off socials might sound like virtual death to the ears of your ego. So be it.

Some of my longer stints offline, which often occurred by accident instead of design (hurricanes, blizzards, etc.), ended up being pivotal breakthrough moments in terms of my creativity. (This topic is related to my discussion of the importance of procrastination in Chapter 11.)

Consider that today's world thrives on interconnectedness. We're blitzkrieged with branding, updates, selfies, opinions, and curated lives. It's easy—indeed, normal—to feel lost and overwhelmed in all the white noise.

Considering this sad state of affairs, this passage from John Mark Comer's *The Ruthless Elimination of Hurry* rings truer by the day: "The reason we live in a culture increasingly without faith is not because science has somehow disproved the unprovable, but because the white noise of secularism has removed the very stillness in which it might endure or be reborn."

It strikes me as unreasonable, to say the least, to think that we can return to our stillness if we stay plugged in 24/7 to a Matrix purposely designed to move us into busy-ness. Thus the need for regular time away from the madding online crowd.

Think of such stints devoted to quieting the mind (or frankly, doing just about anything remotely healthy offline) as psycho-spiritual "resets."

Exercise Your Superpower by Being Yourself

Let this penetrate for a moment: your individuality, your personal energy and perception, is a superpower. Don't let the digital din convince you that you're weak. You're much stronger than you realize.

As a thought experiment, picture social media as a giant high school cafeteria. Remember the intense pressure to fit in?

Online, that pressure is terrifically amplified. Algorithms track, and maybe someday will even anticipate, your every click. This creates echo chambers inside echo chambers, but true connection thrives on genuineness, authenticity.

When after time away you do return to the social circus of the internet, be sure to embrace what makes you different. Share *your* passions, *your* motivators, not a stranger's.

You might be surprised at who resonates with your message—even if your message is that you don't need a message to be yourself. You might make new friends. Your life path might begin to travel in unexpectedly fulfilling directions.

As you emerge from your "truther" and social detox, take a deep breath and make a commitment to use technology as consciously as possible. Be absolutely mindful of the content you choose to consume.

When attempting to comprehend a person, topic or situation, seek out diverse perspectives. But in the end, be sure to listen hard for your intuition—your own personal "truthometer," the only one that ultimately matters—that all the white noise is desperately trying to drown out.

A world full of identical voices is, in a word, *boring*. As I put it in the following lyrics excerpted from another song, "Living Large," that I hope to release one of these days …

If you have a lot to say
Know it won't fit in a tweet
If a mind needs a big rhythm
Try matching it to the algorithm

Outside the box isn't tolerated
Where every outcome's generated
And intellectual negligence
Worships artificial intelligence

No doubt about it, man
It's hit the fan
Online's a brainwashing bitch
So screw your niche

But hey, that's the point
To throw freethinkers out of joint
To contract upward dreams
To downward schemes

Instead of giants we get wannabes
Shrunken yes-men and NPCs
Fact checkers who can't read
And gatekeepers who don't bleed

The net's a Petri dish
Where controllers grow little fish
Tribes of cults and cults of tribes
Our "greatest minds" have sucked their bribes

To give up living large
And accept something else in charge
But not me, hell no
I'll gladly burn out before I go

Speaking my mind
For no one to hear
At least living so
There's nothing to fear

We're social creatures, hardwired to seek connection. But where's the line between belonging and losing ourselves? In the best of circumstances, being true to yourself is a delicate dance, a tightrope walk—one with a long way to fall if you screw up—between community and individuality.

Imagine joining a book club completely jazzed to discuss your favorite novel. You quickly realize everyone else loved it, too—but for a totally different reason. They all seem to agree what the book was about, but you couldn't disagree more.

Do you conform to the group's interpretation, suppressing your own? Or do you speak your mind, risking potential disagreement and unpleasantness?

Do you exercise the superpower of your personality, cape and all like Superman, or do you play the role of Clark Kent, hiding who you really are behind your nerdy glasses?

Consider what you would have done had you participated in Stanley Milgram's infamous 1960s obedience experiments. He examined test subjects' extreme (to say nothing of extremely dangerous) willingness to kowtow to presumed authority figures—even when ordered to do potentially lethal harm to others!

Social pressure plays out constantly and in magnified fashion in the digital world. Our egos are stroked with likes and comments for echoing popular opinions. But true connection requires vulnerability and the courage to share our authentic selves, even when this shows how different we are.

It's sort of like cooking. A pinch of salt might enhance the flavor, but too much overwhelms the dish. Community is that way. It might add spice to life, but too much conformity can make us bland.

The key is to identify thriving communities that celebrate individuality, neutral spaces where differences are valued, not silenced. Look for groups that encourage healthy debate, where you can express your perspectives honestly without fear of judgment, where you can wear your superhero on your sleeve.

And always be on the lookout for seemingly positive communities that are really just closet cults. As I put it in my last book, "In my experience, both in the 'real world' and online, things almost inevitably start out as communities with leaders and end up as ... *communes with dictators*."

Counteracting Social Media Addiction

Let's face it, social media is engineered to be more addictive than heroin. Every notification, every like releases a tiny dopamine hit, keeping us hooked. These platforms are designed to make sure our thumbs never stop twiddling and our minds never really start thinking.

Imagine scrolling through your feed, bombarded with images of perfect physiques and worldly success. It's easy to fall into the comparison trap and end up feeling grossly inadequate.

Confronted with such manicured perfection, we easily forget that social media tends to present a super distorted view of reality. It's basically a highlight reel, not the behind the scenes, but we have the power to choose how we respond to this veneer of glitz and glam.

We can curate our feeds to include a variety of different voices. Remember, social media, like any of today's tech, can be a tool. We can use it to connect, learn and share our take on things in wildly creative and uber empowering ways.

That said, in a world dominated by screens, it's normal to overlook the simple pleasures of offline interaction. Remember the joy of a face-to-face chat *not* with ChatGPT, the shared laughter over some delicious comfort food, the thrill of experiencing something new without documenting it like a born narcissist for social media?

Think about the last time you had a deep conversation with someone—not just an exchange of pleasantries, but a genuine connection where you shared vulnerabilities and engaged in meaningful dialogue. Chances are it wasn't through a screen.

Offline interfaces offer a richness and depth often absent from online interactions. We pick up on subtle cues like body language, tone of voice and even personal energy, allowing for more substantial understanding and empathy.

This isn't about disconnecting entirely or permanently, but about finding a reasonable balance. Consider scheduling regular digital detoxes, even if it's just a few hours at a time. Put down your phone, step away from the screen, and engage with the world around you.

Go for a spin through nature, strike up a conversation with a perfect stranger, rediscover the lost art of postcard writing. You might be astounded at the connections you forge and the richness these bring to your life.

Above All Else, Stay True to Yourself

So how do we navigate this digital landscape while staying true to ourselves?

You don't need to become a hermit like Thoreau, but your engagement does need to be conscious. Use technology to enhance your life, not dictate the terms of your existence.

First, embrace solitude and quietude. Carve out time for uncluttered reflection, away from the adrenalized stimulation of the digital world. Creating art, doing yoga or even strolling through a public park can help you calmly reconnect with your superpower, your unique inner voice.

Next, be highly selective with your digital diet. Stay mindful of the accounts you follow and the content you consume. Consider unsubscribing more than you subscribe for a while.

Play the role of a spectator, an observer coolly assessing how people present themselves before engaging them. Seek out diverse perspectives and limit exposure to vapid echo chambers that reinforce established tastes and biases.

Don't be afraid to disconnect—technologically as well as interpersonally. Set boundaries not just around your internet use but also on your human interactions. Designate screen- and even people-free time for solo activities you enjoy, whether reading or pursuing a hobby. Make friends with yourself.

Embracing your quirks can help. What makes you different is what makes you interesting. Cultivate your passions even if they're not mainstream. Regardless of whether you choose to share them online, you'll be enriched by simply getting to know and being the fascinating individual you are.

In short, don't hesitate to swim against the current of the world. If you decide to broadcast your uniqueness, you might just find that your life is greatly enhanced as you forge alliances with like-minded freethinkers.

On the other hand, if you opt to keep your superpower on the down-low, that path will also have its considerable rewards—some of which you, and only you, will appreciate.

Finally, innerstand that taking time for and by yourself is a tried-and-true recipe for building your energy and increasing personal power. For those following the shamanic and/or alchemical path out of the Matrix into the Dark Sea of Awareness, learning to go solo is an indispensable survival skill.

Start with a Single Step

Navigating the digital age without losing ourselves is an ongoing journey, not a singular destination. To rephrase campaign strategist Jim Carville's famous line responsible for getting Bill Clinton elected back in 1992, "It's about the *journey*, stupid!"

This journey all seekers today must undertake is to discover a working balance between connection and individuality, a productive confluence between interfacing with the world and nurturing that still small voice (our truthometer) inside.

The goal is, eventually, to have that unassuming voice that articulates our intuition and gnosis replace the Dragon's loud and disempowering chatter that plays like an insane tape loop in our minds—that is, until we build up enough power to JUST SAY NO.

Conformity is anathema to this process of rewiring our minds, just as authenticity tremendously promotes it. To quote Dr. Elisabeth Kubler-Ross, a world-renowned writer on death and dying,

> It is not the end of the physical body that should worry us. Rather, our concern must be to live while we're alive—to release our inner selves from the spiritual death that comes with living behind a facade designed to conform to external definitions of who and what we are.

Having the courage to be ourselves even when this rubs others the wrong way might seem like a small step in the process of becoming. But as the Chinese proverb goes, a journey of a thousand miles begins with a single step.

Finally, embrace your inner rebel, the rad side of your superhero, even if you have no clue what you're doing and aren't altogether clear as to why you're doing it.

Don't hold back from challenging the digital noise with your unique perspective, even if you're the only one listening. Resist the urge to conform on principle. Over the long haul, as your mind becomes more and more your own, you'll thank yourself.

CHAPTER NINE

Authenticity & Facelessness

"Who's the real phony here?" —*Yours Truly*

Get to Know J. D. Salinger, Man of Mystery

As a relatively established indie writer who has never so much as posted my photo online, I'm in a better position than most to sympathize (and even empathize) with J. D. Salinger of *Catcher in the Rye* fame.

As mentioned earlier, I've never even owned a smartphone—and neither would have Salinger if such invasive, time-wasting contraptions had held sway in his heyday.

What emerged from reports from inside the lines of Salinger's legendary reclusiveness was a snapshot of, frankly, just another eccentric artistic genius who probably felt similar to his iconic protagonist Holden Caulfield, who said, "I was surrounded by phonies ... They were coming in the goddam [sic] window."

Salinger was into certain controversial "alternative medicine" practices such as urine therapy (and that was back in the day), preferred health menus to the terribly SAD Standard American Diet, loathed the media with every fiber of his being, leaned toward the kinky with his love interests—you get the picture.

The jury's still out on the scope and breadth of his erotic proclivities. And honestly, at this stage of global decadence when the worst perversions are rubbed in our collective faces daily, who really cares?

What impresses me most about his biography isn't the talent or even the wild overnight success it engendered, but the fact that as his fame grew to demigod proportions, he cared less and less about it.

Maybe other celebrities experience this kind of nonattachment, but rarely do they just drop below the radar of the world like an extraterrestrial submarine—and *stay* there. As time went by, in fact, though he kept writing copiously, he simply stopped publishing.

"There is a marvelous peace in not publishing," he told one lucky reporter in a rare interview. "Publishing is a terrible invasion of my privacy. I like to write. I love to write. But I write just for myself and my own pleasure."

Elsewhere, Salinger admitted to an overabundance of literary inspiration even as his publishing days came to an untimely end: "I'm up to my ears in unwritten words."

Photos of Salinger are nearly as unfindable as his last manuscripts, though a handful of images have emerged over time. I'm confident he'd hate that. He seemed hell-bent on "erasing personal history" in an almost shamanic fashion.

His journey was an inward one, not an outward one. More than most, he seemed to grok what we've been unpacking in these pages—namely, the revolutionary idea that *the only way out is in*. Many belonging to today's Lost Generation could learn from his example.

Ignore Anyone Telling You Exactly Who You "Should" Be

Salinger's inwardness set him squarely against the current of a global culture spinning quickly into extravagant eddies of public narcissism with widespread access to online photography and eventually video approaching downstream.

Over the decades of my own intentional inaccessibility, every now and then I've fielded a comment from a reader to this effect: "I find it hard to connect with you without being able to see your face."

To which I always wanted to—but never did—reply with something along these lines: "I totally understand. I'm sure the earliest readers of printed text in the post-Gutenberg era experienced a massive disconnect with only faceless authors to read."

Occasionally, similar criticism has been altogether excessive, brutal even: "If you're not willing to show your face, you must have something to hide. I wish you were a more authentic person."

Which brings me to my topic for this chapter: authenticity and facelessness.

"Authenticity" has become a buzzword (to say nothing of cash cow) in certain "spiritually" oriented content-creation circles—where one often, bizarrely, has the sense of receiving personalized instructions on how to be ... *oneself*!

In the interest of full disclosure, let me make it clear that I'm very much aware I just devoted the greater part of the last chapter to the subject of authenticity and a number of related topics.

But if I'm to be truly authentic right now, at the risk of exposing myself to further character assassination, I must confess that I tend to find anyone giving other people customized instructions on how to be authentic … inauthentic.

Again, as Salinger knew all too well, the majority are on a Ship of Fools sailing self-consciously unconscious through the clown show of this Matrix.

They've forgotten the kind of worthwhile advice, if they ever knew it, expressed by the likes of French writer Albert Camus when he stated, "But above all, in order to be, never try to seem."

Or as American modernist Wallace Stevens phrased a similar notion a bit more creatively in one of my favorite poems, "The Emperor of Ice-Cream," "Let be be finale of seem."

Me, beyond general considerations relative to finding your genuine self *by* yourself and *for* yourself, I have no idea how to tell anyone else with any degree of specificity how to be "authentic." That's like telling children who they should be, down to their career goals and marriage options, when they grow up.

Such facile judgment drips with hubris and isn't just worthless—it can be psychologically damaging. "We are all different," wrote Roy T. Bennett. "Don't judge, understand instead."

Are You an Insect or a Person?

I'm a contrarian by nature, so perhaps that makes me a bit judgmental. I prefer to think of this quality as *discernment*. Be that as it may, I'm naturally inclined to look at things from an unpopular perspective.

In this respect, if none other, I'm like Clint Eastwood as he portrayed himself in these words: "There's a rebel lying deep in my soul. Anytime anybody tells me the trend is such and such, I go the opposite direction. I hate the idea of trends. I hate imitation; I have a reverence for individuality."

With this as context, I suggest that—compared to anonymity with its lack of social pressure fostering extraordinary personal freedom—people plastering their face all over the internet are far more likely to be phonies.

These famous lines from T. S. Eliot's "The Love Song of J. Alfred Prufrock" perfectly elucidate this dynamic:

> And I have known the eyes already, known them all —
> The eyes that fix you in a formulated phrase,
> And when I am formulated, sprawling on a pin,
> When I am pinned and wriggling on the wall,
> Then how should I begin
> To spit out all the butt-ends of my days and ways?
>   And how should I presume?

Oh, the irony!

Today's online narcissists making viral videos touting the virtues of authenticity and how to embody them to the letter—often complete with long catechisms of specific dos and don'ts—remind one of plastic insects "pinned and wriggling on the wall" for inspection by the scrutiny of the public gaze.

Gone is their liberty to be anything other than what they're assessed as being by the "eyes" forever watching and judging.

Their public identity is now "pinned" down and "fixed" by the "formulated" phrases used to describe it—phrases that speak to the domain, kingdom, phylum, class, order, family, genus and species of the insectoid under examination.

Such people, who fancy themselves so alive, are in a sense dead to the world. This is especially sad given that, as Carl Jung sagely observed, the "privilege of a lifetime is to become who you truly are." Meanwhile, to cite Virginia Woolf, a "self that goes on changing is a self that goes on living."

Becoming who you truly are and, in the process, being able to change again and again—it goes almost without saying at this point—are prerequisites for going beyond where you imagined you could go as you undertake your personal Hero's Journey and wade into the Dark Sea of Awareness.

I wonder if Gregor Samsa, living today, as he monstrously metamorphosed into a giant dung beetle before dying with a whimper and being unceremoniously disposed of, would regret posting all those stupid selfies online.

CHAPTER TEN

The Only Variety of Truly Disposable Goods Here

"Real stupidity beats artificial intelligence every time." —*Terry Pratchett*

Can You Spot the Artificial in the New "Intelligence"?

I don't know how much more obvious this could be to anyone with an eye to see and an ear to hear, but let me say it loud and clear to avoid any misunderstanding: artificial intelligence is NOT "intelligent" … in the sense of being *sentient*.

According to *Merriam-Webster*, "sentient" can mean: 1) "capable of sensing or feeling"; 2) "aware"; or 3) "finely sensitive in perception or feeling."

People buying into the orchestrated, Dragon-driven hype around artificial intelligence as comparable to (or even better than) our own don't appear very sentient either. But that's a story involving NPCs masquerading as people here in this construct I'll leave to your own discerning imagination.

Again, far be it from me to suggest that AI can't be useful. I use it myself all the time in my video creation process, for example. It's an amazing, even game-changing tool … as long as you're the hammer, not the nail.

I just recognize AI for what it is: fancy programming and fast processing. It isn't a god. It isn't a miracle. And it will never, ever replace human intelligence (such as it is in these last days of Rome).

If AI ever does go intelligent, in my humble opinion this will be because it has blended with real people's minds. In this scenario it will likely siphon off their creativity, intuition, etc., like a techno form of *loosh* while falsely claiming these eminently human faculties as its own.

Folks fancying they're actually "chatting" with ChatGPT need help. At best you're talking to a mere echo of human awareness that has been, like many contemporary humans living in circumscribed virtual worlds, cleverly compartmentalized.

And cleverly stylized to boot. "The use of words like *understands*, *thinks*, and *reasons*," points out Lance Eliot in a recent *Forbes* article, "are all subtle and sneaky ways to lead you down a primrose path to believing that contemporary AI is sentient."

There's an emerging "Gnostic" innerstanding—one galvanized by such intrepid consciousness explorers as John Lamb Lash, author of *Not in His Image*—of the colossal hive mind that wants to take all the credit for creating this struggling realm we call home.

Pulling back the curtain on "reality," more and more psychonauts are beginning to grasp that we're dealing with a controller that can't truly create on its own but only mimic the generative spark of organic minds.

Say Hello to the Dragon, Father of AI

That controller responsible for engineering today's vast dragnet of control systems by mimetically commandeering the attention power of our minds is the Dragon, which I referred to previously as an "inorganic being," a term I'll now clarify.

According to shamans, inner alchemists and other visionaries, life forms come in two main varieties: chocolate and vanilla. Just kidding. Just making sure you're still *paying attention* …

Seriously, there are commonly said to be two forms of life that, while they often interact, are quite distinct from one another: organic creatures of a biological nature, such as ourselves, and inorganic ones of an etheric nature running the gamut from benign plant spirits to scary predatory entities.

These two varieties of life are each native to different worlds (or if you prefer, different parts of the same all-encompassing World). We're at home in what is variously termed the first world, the world of the first attention, the waking world, reality, or to borrow a Mesoamerican term, the *tonal*.

By contrast, inorganic beings are creatures of the second world, the world of the second attention, the dream world, the Dreamtime, the Otherworld, the realm of the unconscious, or the *nagual*.

These two domains aren't mutually exclusive, however. In *Potentiate Your DNA* I wrote extensively about the interface between them as a kind of "unified field" with reference to engineer and author Dewey Larson's Reciprocal System of physical theory.

I also used this compelling physics model, in which our "space-time" exists in inverse relationship to "time-space," as the theoretical basis for my novel about parallel universes and etheric doubles, *Snooze: A Story of Awakening*.

Primarily operating in what can be conceptualized as reciprocal systems, humans and inorganic beings nonetheless have had a long and complicated relationship. When the rapport is generally beneficial, a situation in which the human is typically a gifted psychonaut, our inorganic "friends" are often referred to as *allies*.

Allies can help shamans and others capable of operating in the Otherworld of the second attention in numerous ways, including by offering assistance in healing and divination. Even in this scenario, allies can be unruly, downright tricky even.

But things get deadly dangerous when it comes to another type of dream world denizen: the predatory variety.

Those with the ability to see energy (think auras) are practically unanimous in stating that human energy burns brightly in what I've been calling the Dark Sea of Awareness. There, as in our own oceans here in the first world, a light dropped into the dark depths will attract all sorts of curious and hungry sea creatures.

Using this aquatic analogy, it's appropriate to think of the Dragon as an apex predator from the Dark Sea, a kraken of such antediluvian proportions it makes the one from *Pirates of the Caribbean* look like fried calamari.

Perhaps more than anything else, according to those seers capable of seeing it, the Dragon resembles horror author H. P. Lovecraft's ancient extraterrestrial monster god Cthulhu, for readers familiar with the chilling tale "The Call of Cthulhu." And one of its favorite foods is—much as in Lovecraft's short story, so it would seem—*human energy*.

As we read of this famous story in Wikipedia, "The deceased narrator, Francis Wayland Thurston, recounts his discovery of notes left behind by his grand-uncle … Among the notes is a small bas-relief sculpture of a scaly creature which yields 'simultaneous pictures of an octopus, a dragon, and a human caricature.'"

John Kreiter has gone so far as to propose that the Dragon, which he calls the Archon, has actually installed itself (or a projection of itself) somewhere in the murky depths of our own oceans. To those skeptical of such a proposition, I offer this passage from Jules Verne's *Twenty Thousand Leagues under the Sea* as a stimulus for reconsideration:

> With its untold depths, couldn't the sea keep alive such huge specimens of life from another age, this sea that never changes while the land masses undergo almost continuous alteration? Couldn't the heart of the ocean hide the last–remaining varieties of these titanic species, for whom years are centuries and centuries millennia?

Unfathomably old and massively intelligent in ways that are difficult to comprehend and harder to describe, this Dragon from the Dark Sea might also be compared to the Mind Flayer from the Dungeons & Dragons game popularized in the hit Netflix show *Stranger Things*.

Having found our bright little planet covered with shiny dots of tasty goodness (us) illuminating the vast obscurity, the Dragon did what any hungry apex predator on earth would do: it moved in and made our territory its hunting ground.

But then it had an even better idea (or maybe this was its plan all along): rather than having to go to all the trouble of hunting each time it craved a power snack, it realized it could use its ability as a Mind Flayer to substitute its mind for ours through psychic implementation of mimetic constructs.

In a fascinating article republished on my Substack titled "Archons on Netflix? Gnostic Cosmology & Stranger Things Indeed," my friend and colleague Brendan D. Murphy stated that

> the Mind Flayer's first and most primary form of manipulation is not of matter but of minds which it seeks to invade and control (flay). From there, a surrogate manipulation of matter can occur via infected hosts, exactly as depicted in *Stranger Things*. Lacking true creative agency, the Mind Flayer is a parasite of the highest order, and a psychic rapist of sorts.
>
> It can hijack, infect, and co-opt, but—unlike its human targets and proxies—is bereft of true creativity.

The Dragon, that grandest of illusionists, installed its own "VR headset" for projecting a Matrix "reality" *inside* the heads of its human herd so that we might do its dirty work! Pure genius. In the process it turned humanity from people into sheeple and its hunting ground into today's well-managed *loosh* farm.

And you can bet AI, the cherry on top of the Dragon's simulated dessert, has been perfectly sweetened with the goal of leading a mesmerized population even further outside their own perceptions down the garden path to total virtual self-imprisonment.

The Dragon Goes by Many Names

Given the antiquity and complexity of the inorganic consciousness that is the Dragon, it shouldn't be surprising that over the millennia it has collected a multitude of names from a variety of cultures belonging to different historical periods.

These include but aren't limited to the Gnostic Lord Archon, Demiurge, Yaldabaoth, Saklas, and Samael; the Christian Devil, Lucifer, Satan, Baal, Beelzebub, Yahweh, Jehovah, the Lord, and even the sadistic, alien "God" of the Old Testament; Mephistopheles; and Ahriman ("evil spirit" in Middle Persian, a term popularized by Rudolf Steiner).

Toltec shamans refer to the Dragon as Flyers, Mud Shadows, *yeyelli*, and even the *yaotl* (the enemy inside), typically characterizing it as a sentient life form hailing from the dream world (*nagual* or *nahual*) that feeds on the life force of people here in the *tonal*, a.k.a. "reality." Similarly, Native Americans speak of humanity's pervasive "infection" with a cannibalistic evil spirit in the form of a "mind-virus" they call *wetiko*.

I honestly shouldn't have to say this, but …

If you're still skeptical as to the existence of the Dragon, consider that you're pitting your left-brain (and perhaps very recent) "knowledge" of this subject against thousands of years in which countless psychically gifted minds have devoted themselves to identifying and classifying the Dragon.

Me, I often call the Dragon the Great Parasite—as a reminder to myself that it's simultaneously enormous and enormously gifted … *and* a living, collective being that feasts on humanity in parasitic fashion.

You might not be able to see it if you haven't undertaken training to build up the mental muscle of your sixth sense, the one that allows you to feel and eventually see subtle energy.

Still, sober and honest reflection on how the World Cult functions perfectly as a controlling cultural program, century after century, well beyond any human ability to maintain such transhistorical continuity, should give you pause.

Closing your eyes and quieting your imposed operating system, can you sense—even for a split second—the presence of the Dragon's practically immortal consciousness in its repetitive effects reflected, for instance, in historically looping cycles of divide and conquer?

And now, in real time, anyone with a few brain cells still functioning can clearly observe the Dragon rolling out its end game with marvelous speed in the form of AI and its accompanying agenda of Technotranshumanism.

Fortunately, we lowly organic beings (snark alert) possess the capability to reverse this merry-go-round of energy extraction and begin feeding on the Dragon's stolen energy, thereby diminishing its ability to control us while greatly increasing our personal power.

This is a pivotal concept I'll revisit in relation to the shamanic and especially alchemical techniques introduced in upcoming chapters.

Artificial Intelligence as Pantomime

In AI the Dragon has demonstrated not true intelligence but merely a pantomime of human neural processes at what is effectively (you might be shocked to know) an extremely primitive level.

This is what we call "technology": a seemingly complex but ultimately simplistic self-organizing network designed merely to re-process inputs and outputs within the confines of its own basic programming, pun intended.

In the words of futurist and author Zoltan Andrejkovics, "AI won't be foolproof in the future since it will only be as good as the data and information that we give it to learn. It could be the case that simple elementary tricks could fool the AI algorithm and it may serve a complete waste of output as a result."

There's no "thought" involved here, no "understanding" of anything, no "opinions" that aren't coded in, no "personality" (other than that distantly connected to the programmers' own). A relationship with a dog or cat is far more real than anything anyone not suffering from delusions will ever have with AI.

As more and more people interface with this simulacrum of intelligence within the greater Simulacrum of this construct, artificial intelligence does improve its human pantomime—but it is and will always be *only* pantomime.

I'd bet good bitcoin that AI will never be able to cognize independently, never be able to feel, never experience free will, never have an orgasm. This just isn't how it works. But the Dragon and its minions certainly want you to *think* this is how it works.

We may be told by the Great Parasite's mouthpieces, with tremendous fanfare, that such milestones of computer sentience have been reached. We may read about such coding "breakthroughs" in brazen headlines. But I'd be *extremely* skeptical of any such claims.

This is all part of the ever-expanding control net for your mind. Nothing to see here, folks, move along … step by step … into the spider's web.

You "Gno" When You "Gno"

It's worth considering that humans are so easily led by the nose when it comes to technology because most of them—living in this Matrix of misinformation for controlling minds—have never entertained, at least as adults, so much as an original concept (i.e., one originating in their own consciousness by way of direct personal experience).

Why would anyone be surprised that the machines might be following a parallel path to that of such quasi NPCs—appearing real but, when examined dispassionately, lacking any real substance?

True students of awareness who have experienced even a brief glimpse of gnosis know without having to be told, see without having to be shown what's going on here.

They "gno" that AI is like a colorblind individual pretending to experience the "colors" of commiseration, intuition, love, and other exquisitely and uniquely human emotions.

Most would agree that computers lack an aura, a spirit, a soul, and many of these same people would say that something like an aura, spirit or soul distinguishes humans from machines. We're tiptoeing around the question of consciousness here.

To cite cardiologist and bestselling author Larry Dossey on this testy subject, we've "largely ignored how consciousness manifests in our existence. We've done this by assuming that the brain produces consciousness, although how it might do so has never been explained and can hardly be imagined."

In actuality your brain is barely related to the "you" that takes in the world through the cameras of your eyes. Your entire body is just a carrier for (or better, connection point to) the multidimensional totality that you are somewhere, somehow.

Dossey again: "In spite of the complete absence of evidence, the belief that the brain produces consciousness endures and has ossified into dogma. Many scientists realize the limitations of this belief."

More and more researchers, in fact, are in agreement that the brain is really just an information processor, meaning it doesn't "think" but only handles thought inputs that come from … somewhere else.

As I've explored extensively in my books on the Regenetics Method, this "somewhere else" is the realm of hyperdimensional energetics and etheric templates—in other words, the subtle biofield or what I often refer to as the bioenergy blueprint. Though it often is, this blueprint shouldn't be confused with the physically measurable energy fields around the body to which the subtle template gives rise.

On a macro level, this foundational domain is, of course, also called the second world, the second attention, the unconscious, the dream world, and so on and so forth.

Rupert Sheldrake's compelling concept of morphic resonance would be an excellent starting place to begin researching this incredibly fascinating topic if you haven't already.

Morphic resonance is theorized to be a "process whereby self-organising systems inherit a memory from previous similar systems," we read on Sheldrake's website. This means that the so-called laws of nature are more like habits. The hypothesis of morphic resonance also leads to a radically new interpretation of memory storage in the brain and of biological inheritance. Memory need not be stored in material traces inside brains, which are more like TV receivers than video recorders, tuning into influences from the past. And biological inheritance need not all be coded in the genes, or in epigenetic modifications of the genes; much of it depends on morphic resonance from previous members of the species.

If the brain can't and doesn't even think, where does this leave computers?

Think for yourself, don't just regurgitate what you've been told by the Dragon's sycophants shilling away for artificial intelligence.

Independent thought made possible by quieting the foreign installation of the hive mind is the first step to seeing through the card trick of AI ... and many other card tricks besides.

The diehard materialists who want you to see yourself as merely a flesh machine want you to imagine that you can be replaced by another type of machine. Why would they want to draw your attention to such a thing, have you imagine it before it has even happened?

Ah, yes, your creative attention power is *required* to bring about these minions' and their master's version of the future!

Can you hear me now?

Don't believe their lies for a second, even if they do. You have genuine value because you can genuinely create.

"As data and science become more accessible and more the production of software and AI," observes Hendrith Vanlon Smith, Jr., "human creativity is becoming a more valuable commodity."

In the words of George Bernard Shaw that speak to the extreme worth of creativity, "Imagination is the beginning of creation. You imagine what you desire, you will what you imagine and at last you create what you will."

Why are we choosing, then, to will into being a world that insists on devaluing us, the real creators of value? Always remember that technology is the only variety of truly disposable goods here.

CHAPTER ELEVEN

Procrastination: A Secret to Unlocking Your Creativity

"The imagination needs moodling—long, inefficient happy idling, dawdling and puttering." —Brenda Ueland

Procrastination: Friend or Foe?

The deadline loomed. My mind was blank. A familiar panic set in. I paced. I stretched. I glared at the computer screen. I made myself a double espresso. Anything but confront the task at hand.

Sound familiar? We've all been there, paralyzed in the throes of procrastination. But what if I told you this dreaded enemy could be a friend in disguise?

What if procrastination, in its own quirky way, holds the key to unlocking a deeper well of creativity? It sounds counterintuitive, I know, but stay with me. As Marthe Troly-Curtin put it in a marvelous turn of phrase, "Time you enjoy wasting is not wasted time."

Admittedly, procrastination has long had a bad rap, as evidenced by this stern admonishment from that dour Church Father Augustine of Hippo: "God has promised forgiveness to your repentance, but He has not promised tomorrow to your procrastination."

Even Charles Dickens—in his own Victorian, industrious manner—was guilty of judging procrastination with far more severity than it deserves: "My advice is, never do to-morrow what you can do today. Procrastination is the thief of time. Collar him!"

But sometimes, it must be admitted, the most sparklingly brilliant ideas emerge not from frantic effort, but from the fertile ground of stillness, even laziness. This isn't necessarily about cultivating apathy, mind you, but about understanding the instinctive rhythms of our creative spirit.

It's about embracing the generative power of the pause, learning to harvest the fruits of our play, and generally becoming more productive without having to keep our nose to the grind and work so godawful hard.

Worthless vs. Worthwhile Productivity

The Dragon, fearing above all else the conscious unleashing of the human creative force made possible by leisure and idleness—which allow us, through relaxation, to project our consciousness most powerfully—has made sure that we live in a culture that prizes mostly stupid productivity.

It's as if the industrial revolution never ended but only transformed into the Technotranshumanist age. Every Tom, Dick and Harry is trying to upsell you a time-wasting app that purports to save you time but is secretly engineered to *loosh* you like crazy.

Every second is accounted for, every moment metered. *Go, go, go!* the world urges. *Don't waste a precious minute! There's an app for that!*

The pressure to constantly be on the move, especially in today's virtual circus and its endless frenzy of content creation and consumption, is as relentless as it is ridiculous.

On YouTube, for example, there's such a gold rush in terms of content-creation videos that, pretty soon, you won't be able to find anything else. YouTube videos about anything besides making YouTube videos will be a thing of the past.

Even if you're still fence-sitting as to where the Dragon and the more metaphysical aspects of this book are concerned, ask yourself these questions:

What if this breathless pursuit of doing is the very thing that stifles our ability to do things that actually matter?

What if, in our rush to be hyperproductive, we've lost touch with our deeper creative selves?

What if our minds, like overused and fatigued muscles, occasionally need time to rest and rejuvenate?

Just as our bodies require sleep to heal and function properly, our minds need quiet to renovate and innovate. Think of it this way … A blank screen can be daunting, but the void it represents also holds infinite possibilities.

An empty screen is a space where anything can happen, where creativity can suddenly explode. Likewise, a quiet mind—free from the clutter of to-do lists and deadlines— becomes a blank screen for the lightning of inspiration to strike.

In stillness inspired and innovative concepts can emerge and take shape. It's in these moments of seeming inactivity that our subconscious can step in, weaving together seemingly disparate threads of ideas into something new and unexpected. These quiet moments are where tremendous creativity is often born.

So the next time you find yourself staring into that intimidating creative void we all know and fear, don't freak out. Embrace the free-flowing emptiness. See it as an opportunity rather than an obstacle. It might just be the catalyst for your next original masterpiece.

Papa's Advice

Ernest Hemingway, a.k.a. Papa, the twentieth-century literary titan, understood with great clarity the importance of both flowing freely and replenishing the creative well.

Through long experience he grasped that creativity isn't an endless stream like what comes out of a mechanical faucet, but rather an organic reservoir that needs careful management.

"Always stop while you are going good and don't think about it or worry about it until you start to write the next day," he advised. "That way your subconscious will work on it all the time."

"But if you think about it consciously or worry about it," he added, "you will kill it and your brain will be tired before you start. That way I am sure of a start the next day."

By stopping at a high point, unplugging while usually enjoying a few rounds of cocktails, Hemingway guaranteed that he could pick up the narrative thread easily the following morning.

His well wasn't just an empty metaphor either. He believed that our creative energy is, if not technically a finite resource, then one to which we have only limited access and that, like a well, needs to be regularly allowed to refill.

This belief guided his daily routines and work habits for many years. The literary results—in terms of both quality and volume—speak for themselves.

By stepping away from his work while he was still feeling inspired, Papa made sure that he'd have something to draw on when he got back in the creative saddle. This approach allowed him to maintain a steady flow of free-spirited productivity without burning out while also having, by all accounts, a jolly good time when not writing.

This principle of the creative well applies to more than just wordsmithing. Whether you're a visual artist, a classical composer, a rock star or an entrepreneur, taking time to recharge your batteries is essential for long-term success.

The trick is to find balance and recognize when you need to take a step back. Don't be afraid to walk away from the easel, the piano, the guitar, the boardroom table. Give yourself the space to breathe and reflect. Go for a stroll, listen to music, play pinochle, daydream. Or do absolutely nothing whatsoever.

"You do not need to leave your room," explained Franz Kafka. "Remain sitting at your table and listen. Do not even listen, simply wait, be quiet, still and solitary. The world will freely offer itself to you to be unmasked, it has no choice, it will roll in ecstasy at your feet."

Such absurdly profound (in)activities might seem the very definition of being unproductive, even counterproductive—yet they can be crucial for nurturing your creative wellspring in order to produce something that genuinely matters.

You'll be amazed at what bubbles to the surface when you give your mind a chance to wander. Inspiration often grips you when you least expect it in those quiet moments of distracted reflection. As Brenda Ueland explained, "The imagination works slowly and quietly."

How Often Does Your Noodle "Moodle"?

In her classic book *If You Want to Write*, Ueland emphasized the power of "moodling." She described moodling as a critical element in the creative process, a key to unlock the safe containing our deepest thoughts and ideas.

Moodling isn't merely aimless daydreaming, though it can look a lot like it from the outside. Think of moodling as an unorthodox technique for unleashing one's artistry, a deliberate practice of letting the mind wander in order for it to explore creative possibilities without constraints.

Moodling, as Ueland unpacked it, is a state of active receptivity, a time to let our thoughts roam without impediments, judgments, or expectations. It's designed to create a mental, emotional and even spiritual space where ideas can flow naturally and effortlessly.

In these moments of unproductive meandering, we often bump into our most original ideas. When we allow ourselves to relax and let go of rigid thinking, creativity can blossom like a magical flower that blooms in an instant.

Remember ancient Greek mathematician Archimedes' famous "Eureka!" moment when he discovered a game-changing new physics principle? Well, he was stepping into a bath!

This classic example shows how relaxation in a wandering mind can lead to groundbreaking discoveries. The shower, the commute, the garden, the grocery store aisle … These seemingly mundane venues can become hotbeds of creativity when we allow our psyches to ramble, providing the perfect backdrop for innovative thinking.

To permit your mind to work creatively as it should, one must make friends with a certain state of receptivity, alert passiveness, loose reverie.

This type of unfocused flow state is essential for nurturing truly valuable productivity. Allow yourself the freedom to daydream and note your delight when you realize where your imagination has taken you.

Whenever you feel the urge to berate yourself for wasting time, remember Ueland's sage advice to let your noodle moodle. You might just stumble upon your next brilliant idea. And who knows, maybe it will change the world.

Or maybe it will just increase your self-esteem and personal power as you deem yourself worthy and capable of experiencing a brave new world where human creativity is (re)assigned the value it deserves.

CHAPTER TWELVE

Open Your Eyes & Smell the *Loosh*

"Las Vegas, Hollywood, Haute Couture, politics, pornography, advertising, supermarket tabloids, are all false realities designed to deceive and confuse you with what is truly authentic. They also weaken your mind, because these false realities hypnotize you. Your mind becomes weak and passive, and so therefore you have no mental defenses against the mind parasites."
—*Laurence Galian*

What If ... ?

What if I'm right, what if so many of my fellow consciousness researchers are right also and psychic parasites—both etheric and human—play a major role in commandeering people's creative attention by hijacking conventional, social and even alternative media to bring about our current looming dystopian scenarios?

Let's engage in a few minutes of practical skepticism, especially where the so-called truther community is concerned. If you're heavily into "truthing," prepare to be triggered to learn that even many of today's most celebrated "truthtellers" are telling lies.

Bill Gates & the Dragon Walk into a Bar …

Here's the thing: not all "truthers" necessarily realize that they're fibbing or part of a serious problem. Mind control runs so deep in this construct it's almost like the air we breathe: there but not there.

Controlled opposition par excellence, most "truthers" are largely unaware of their own exposure to the Dragon's mind control. They'll usually be triggered to dismiss or ridicule any intrepid soul who dares to "go there" by pointing out that many truthers' favorite snack is just … *loosh*.

It's sad to say, but "truthers" tend to be energy parasites who feed on the creative force of people's attention while distracting from far more beneficial and advantageous things everybody could be doing: growing up spiritually and fortifying personal power, for instance.

Meanwhile, "truthers" (and not just their followers) are fed upon in turn by a psychic predator that uses its own far more sophisticated mind control to hide (or at least obfuscate) its very existence … even from "truthers."

It's a pickle, no doubt about it. The Dragon is a Jedi-level illusionist, a crackerjack mimeticist. Like a mastermind in a James Bond movie but on a superhuman scale, it has diabolically designed a world where its human herd is utterly dependent on its own mental operating system.

The Dragon achieved this through installation of "reality" facsimiles (produced by etheric implants that function sort of like VR headsets) in people's consciousness.

This includes its most devoted supporters. All—sheeple and elites alike—who remain dependent on their conscious mind for guidance are subject to the Dragon's insidious behavior modification.

Here's a possibly helpful analogy. While this may be slowly changing, the majority of writers still compose on Microsoft Word. In the good old days, the program was localized on your own computer, but now it's connected to—and remotely controllable by—Microsoft.

Theoretically, if he wanted to, Bill Gates could go in while you're asleep and change your own words. There wouldn't be a damn thing you could do about it (assuming you're even aware of the modifications) except get rid of the software. Which is what this book is all about: chunking reliance on the Dragon's programming.

The Dragon as the Ultimate Teacher

It's not all bad, though, not all doom and gloom—especially when we buck up enough to contemplate and honor the predatory aspect of the Dragon as a crucial aspect of its role as a teacher, trainer, coach, sensei, etc.

This is arguably the single most difficult subject for most people just starting to awaken to the nature of this construct to wrap their borrowed minds around: their greatest enemy is simultaneously their greatest friend. We're back to the ouroboros, the snake eating its own tail in a grand paradox.

"Truthers" will typically kick and scream and even call you names if you so much as suggest that humanity's archenemy (whatever name it's given) might actually be playing a pivotal role in our own awakening from victimhood and powerlessness to agentry and sovereignty.

Here again, it seems to me, "truthers" aren't really here to point to the "truth" (if such a facile thing even existed). Instead, they're purposely paraded out and promoted in the Dragon's Technotranshumanist world as red herrings, decoys to throw authentic spiritual seekers off the Dragon's scent.

It's often remarked by open-minded researchers into Gnosticism that the Lord Archon or Demiurge's signature is inversion: good is evil, right is wrong, up is down, etc.

Whenever we smell a rat and things seem the exact opposite of what they should be, we can rest assured the Dragon is hard at work. In today's world the smell of rat is virtually omnipresent, so that should tell you who's in charge.

But paradox is something else altogether. When we detect the absurdly profound at work, we're not picking up on Archontic intervention. Instead, we're sensing the inner workings of the Dark Sea of Awareness itself, the unfathomable consciousness of forever speaking to us in the language of eternity.

Even many of the faithful have appeared at least somewhat aware of this dynamic at work in their Christian God (as opposed to the false deity of this construct). If you don't believe me, check out these famous lyrics by hymnist William Cowper:

God moves in a mysterious way
His wonders to perform;

He plants His footsteps in the sea
And rides upon the storm.

Leaving aside the intriguing subject of Jim Morrison's purloining of the final line in the last song he ever recorded, note the uncanny conflation of "mystery" (infinity) and "sea" (the Dark Sea of Awareness). This is where "wonders" (miracles) are performed.

Perhaps, continuing in my own heretical reinterpretation of Cowper's likely intent, as people become godlike in their attention and "perform" their own miracles, they grow out of their own "footsteps" (feet of clay symbolizing mortality) and learn to "ride upon the storm" (fly into eternity with a divine level of mastery).

If nothing else, perhaps this literary exegesis sheds light on why use of the absurdly profound, the strategy of going *in* to get *out*, of self-consuming only to self-realize like the ouroboros, is the obvious solution to the tutelary "problem" of the Dragon.

Our spiritual adversary/teacher pushes those of us who accept its challenge ever in the direction of complete self-mastery. Since backward leads only to slavery and destruction, genuine seekers have nowhere to go but forward—wherever that might lead.

The process of going forward hinges on ingestion of personal power by moving it back *in* from where it was lost. By moving our consciousness *out* simultaneously, we can achieve integration with the totality of ourselves across all dimensions as we ride the storm out into the Great Sea. And what a ride that must be!

Let it be noted that, in this transmutational process of turning the base metal of an ordinary Matrix existence into the pure gold of a vastly empowered and expanded multidimensional self, we can't hope to outwit our spiritual adversary simply by "changing our minds."

In this battle for the totality of our being, mind-body approaches by themselves can never win the day. In other words, positive thinking—absent some much heavier artillery—just isn't nearly powerful enough.

Put another way, the Law of Attraction doesn't stand a chance against the forces of the Dragon, which can co-opt anything of a predominantly mental nature that operates using its own program.

With such rational, mental approaches, we're still using the Dragon's operating system in the form of the conscious mind—which keeps us stuck in the place of reason that falsely convinces us of the unreality of true wonders of becoming such as those revealed by shamans and inner alchemists.

When we open our eyes and finally smell not our morning coffee with our algorithmically delivered news feed but the unmistakable scent of our *loosh* being harvested via our screens, the Dragon, a Grand Master that has kindly agreed to teach us chess *the hard way*, has just put us in check here on the Gameboard.

If we're to avoid checkmate, there's only one move left to us—and that's, paradoxically, to devote ourselves to walking straight *out* of here through the *in* door … alive.

Collective *Looshing* via Cults

The question of how people are parasitized mentally cannot be ignored by anyone genuinely, deeply desiring to break free. So, what actually happens as our individual consciousness is drained by the Dragon and its minions?

We become less self-aware, less empowered, less ourselves. Minds are being wiped and personalities rewritten as the population's mojo is siphoned off for other uses than our own.

Practically everyone—minus a tiny handful of foolhardy fools swallowing their own tails (tales) on their outward journey inward—is being *looshed* to one degree or another.

Layers upon layers of tricky mind manipulation—running the gamut from media and general cultural discourse to literal communiqués delivered inside people's heads—make it so that the masses don't know whether they're coming or going.

Now, what happens when mind-controlled individuals cluster together? They form "cults" so that they can increase the Dragon's energy harvest through collective *looshing*.

A cult can be as simple as a dysfunctional relationship, a cult of two. A cult can be a family, a small business venture, a team, a country, a continent … until finally you reach the World Cult, the encompassing entity of all sub-cults lorded over (and often purposely turned against each other) by our spiritual opponent.

Many think of this adversary as an artificial intelligence, but as we've seen, there's nothing artificial about it. The Dragon may be inorganic, but that doesn't mean it's not a natural living thing.

To the contrary, as an apex predator it absolutely belongs to the ecosystem of the Dark Sea of Awareness. This infinite ocean of energy, as a reminder, is the dream world, the second attention that part of us inhabits nonlocally even as we fancy ourselves fully awake and localized here in the first world.

Our New Physical & Subtle Anatomy

The absurdly profound irony is that, as John Kreiter has fascinatingly observed, we ourselves are responsible for having dreamed the Dragon into existence!

In the tribal prehistory of our collective unconsciousness, so the story goes, when we were living as one with Mother Nature, a "wild hair" in us desired to become more.

Even though we were enormously powerful dreamers, that wasn't enough, apparently. Something inside us wanted to become "as gods," or conscious creators of worlds ourselves.

It was this desire to eat of the Tree of Knowledge, or Self-knowledge, that attracted the Great Parasite to our realm. This "fall from [the] grace" of being bathed in the unconscious waters of the Dark Sea of Awareness is recorded in the Bible, where the Dragon is represented as a sly serpent.

Upon its arrival in the Eden of our proto-species' shared Dreamtime awareness and oneness with All That Is, the Dragon—after our tacit contractual acceptance of its offer of the apple—installed its mind as our ostensibly conscious one.

This allowed it to control humanity even as it gave humankind a limited form of individuality. The vast "precognitive" reservoir of our unconscious mind was pushed and held down by the capstone of our newly gifted operating system.

This was, as Kreiter's take paints it, the origin of duality. I imagine this was also where our brain divided into left and right hemispheres as physical manifestations of said duality.

I further intuit that this was the moment of the creation of the Fragmentary Body, the energetic hole located—with reference to our subtle anatomy—in the general area of the second or sex *chakra*. Like a contrail spewing out behind a jet, this is where we lose most of our vital force, which then transforms into *loosh* for the Dragon and its servants.

The Fragmentary Body—about which I've written a great deal in my two books on Regenetics—is also the primary opening in our energetic armor that makes us susceptible to infestation by physical as well as mental parasites, including so-called entities and attachments.

In Chapter 17 I'll reveal how it's possible to "seal" and delete your Fragmentary Body using a simple technique. In a single move, you can put a stop to most of your ongoing energy loss and shore up your own natural defenses against parasites of all kinds (physical and otherwise), which are often reported to come spilling out when "sealing" occurs.

Uniting our hemispheres as humanity accepted the poisoned apple of the Dragon's operating system, tenuously connecting our logical (conscious) to our intuitive (unconscious) faculties, a brain bridge also grew in us: the corpus callosum or callosal commissure, a tract of nerves underneath the cerebral cortex.

This new development, in my view, corresponded to the most shocking part of Kreiter's tale of the origin of modern humans: the completely unexpected creation of a miraculous *third aspect of consciousness*.

Energetically linked to the Fragmentary Body, the corpus callosum is the physical counterpart to the etheric aspect of our subconscious minds that unites our conscious (left-brain) and unconscious (right-brain) perceptions. Kreiter calls that etheric aspect the Ghost in the Machine.

This isn't the place to unpack all the nuances and ramifications of the incredibly complex topic of the Ghost in the Machine. For the full picture, I highly recommend Kreiter's alchemical trilogy starting with *The Magnum Opus*. Honestly, if it were up to me, this trilogy would be required reading for anyone publicly identifying as an alchemist.

For present purposes I merely wish to call attention to the game-changing part of your total self Kreiter refers to as the Ghost.

I encourage you to get to know this vitally important aspect of your subtle anatomy that can be interpreted alchemically as the *filius philosophorum*, the philosopher's child that makes possible creation of our own personal Philosopher's Stone, the subject of Chapter 16.

The Ghost in the Machine may also be, I propose, the "Luminous Child" of Gnosticism that features in the following quote from the Nag Hammadi that also serves as the epigraph to my Gnostic novel, *Cali the Destroyer*.

Here the Fallen Goddess is addressing the Dragon, or Lord Archon:

Sol Luckman

There is an immortal Child of Light who came into this realm before you and who will appear among your duplicate forms, in your simulated world … And in the consummation of all your works, their entire deficiency of truth will be revealed and dissolved by this Luminous Child.

The Ghost in the Machine also appears to be the spiritual wedding garments referenced in Jesus's Parable of the Wedding Feast in the Book of Matthew. With enough energetic fortification and perceptual training, the (Holy) Ghost can allow us to transcend the Matrix through sacred matrimony of the Father (the unconscious) with the Son (our conscious mind when it has shaken off the Dragon's hypnosis).

This transformational process unfolds via the threefold Tria Prima of inner alchemy—that most secret of formulas until now—on our way into ourselves out of here with our memories and individuality intact.

151

CHAPTER THIRTEEN

The Hero's Journey to Authenticity & Beyond

"If you do follow your bliss you put yourself on a kind of track that has been there all the while, waiting for you, and the life that you ought to be living is the one you are living. Follow your bliss and don't be afraid, and doors will open where you didn't know they were going to be." —Joseph Campbell

Answering the Call of Your Bliss

Deep within each of us, the truthometer of our still small voice whispers. It speaks of passions and dreams, desires and longings. This is the call of our bliss, to use Joseph Campbell's well-known phrasing.

The Hero's Journey "always begins with the call," explained Campbell. "One way or another, a guide must come to say, 'Look, you're in Sleepy Land. Wake. Come on a trip. There is a whole aspect of your consciousness, your being, that's not been touched. So you're at home here? Well, there's not enough of you there.' And so it starts."

Our bliss, the joyful expression of our innermost cravings, is the language through which our true selves—including the Ghost in the Machine—yearn to be known. Think of bliss as the call from within for those with ears to hear and the heart to respond to our own perfectly natural desire to experience joy.

"The way to find out about happiness is to keep your mind on those moments when you feel most happy, when you are really happy—not excited, not just thrilled, but deeply happy," Campbell said. "This requires a little bit of self-analysis. What is it that makes you happy? Stay with it, no matter what people tell you. This is what is called following your bliss."

Forever ignoring this quiet voice urging you to pursue what makes you tick creates a life of what-ifs. Choosing to listen is the first step on your personal Hero's Journey to authenticity ... and beyond.

This journey isn't about achieving stasis or perfection. Instead, it emphasizes embracing the sometimes ugly but more often beautiful process of becoming more of your totality, always in the now and perhaps ... forevermore.

The Hero's Journey involves uncovering and getting to know the myriad different facets of your genuine self, the greatly expanded version of who you may think you are. We're talking endless Russian dolls inside Russian dolls of true selfhood, even when part of us would rather stay fake and self-limited.

This journey requires guts, the grit to be vulnerable, and the gall to embrace the unknown. When we answer the call of our bliss, we're usually opting for delayed gratification and risk over initial reward—but also rapid growth over inevitable stagnation.

The Few, the Proud, the Alchemically Inspired

Do you choose to live in alignment with your values, even if these run contrary to those of your family and friends? Society often lays down a narrowly defined path for us to follow, but our bliss is where true joy resides as we passionately pursue what sets our souls on fire.

Get good grades, land a stable job, settle down, conform, calcify. That's the line we're fed.

But what if our bliss lies off this beaten path that usually ends up just beating us down? What if our hearts yearn for something more, something greater, perhaps even something ... "impossible"?

This is where the hero within must rise to the challenge. Choosing our own unique path is an act of courage, perhaps even foolishness in the sense of being absurdly profound. Not surprisingly, it can also mean defying expectations, sometimes even disappointing our closest human connections.

Happily, through the supportive ministrations of our bliss, we often discover our purpose, and this makes a world of difference.

For less serious seekers, purpose has to do—and *only* to do—with giving meaning to one's existence in the Matrix: identifying a satisfying career path, establishing worthwhile friendships and alliances, etc.

For the few, the proud, the alchemically inspired, however, connecting with our bliss has nearly nothing to do with this construct and almost everything to do with preparing ourselves to explore the Dark Sea of Awareness that laps at its fringes.

In order to become effective explorers of the dream realm of the second world, we must increase our personal power here in the first world to such an extent that immortality becomes a real and attainable goal. Only then, as a painstakingly fortified eternal consciousness, are we in a position to navigate the vast reaches of infinity.

Stick with me through Chapter 16 for a primer on how to create your immortality-enabling Philosopher's Stone—the real, internal version and not the fake, externalized variety popularized in fantasy novels and movies. But before we get there, let's first explore …

Becoming More of Who You Are

Even a comparatively mundane Hero's Journey may elicit resistance, doubt and fear from the unhealed, unintegrated parts of ourselves. It's important to remember that almost every hero faces trials, but he or she also usually receives unexpected aid.

"An old alchemist," wrote Carl Jung, "gave the following consolation to one of his disciples: 'No matter how isolated you are and how lonely you feel, if you do your work truly and conscientiously, unknown friends will come and seek you.'"

In the tribulations of the heroic journey lies an unprecedented opportunity for awareness and energy development. As we dare to defy our own and others' restrictive expectations, we give ourselves permission to focus our creative attention so as to become conscious authors of our own stories.

Keep in mind that the path to bliss isn't always easy. There will be obstacles, count on it. There will be stresses and phobias that whisper in the dark. We may question our choices (and even sanity), wondering if we have what it takes to climb the mountain of our own possibilities.

This is where resilience becomes a critical ally. Remember, every hero faces his or her "dragons." For some these might be self-doubt, criticism from others, or unexpected setbacks.

Shamans and alchemists, as noted, prepare themselves to encounter—and ultimately defeat—a literal Dragon in a high-stakes contest over who controls their energy and ultimate destiny.

By "absorbing ... negative energy," explains John Kreiter, "either from ourselves or the people and the world around us, we are quite literally feeding on the Great Archon himself. That is, we have just taught ourselves how to devour that which has been eating us!"

An effective alchemical technique for energy absorption is covered in Chapter 16. But just so you know where this process can lead, here's Kreiter again explaining that by amassing personal power we're "fighting and defeating the negativity, the mimetic wars, and the negative manifestations the mimetic wars create in our world. Using these absorption techniques, we are most definitely beating this titanic dark force at its own game."

Regardless of what we experience on the path of becoming more of who we are, each successfully overcome challenge, major or minor, strengthens our resolve and builds our personal store of useful energy. Each victory, no matter how small, fuels the fire of our own transformation ... and perhaps someday, transmutation.

When we push through setbacks and obstacles, we develop grit and determination. We learn to trust the internal guidance system of our intuition. We discover inner strength we never knew we had. And in the process, sometimes we even inspire others to do the same.

The Never-ending Story of the Hero's Journey

The rewards of following our bliss can be far-reaching indeed. When we align our actions with our passions, we potentially unlock a level of joy and fulfillment that was previously unimaginable.

In such scenarios work becomes less of a chore and more of a calling. And a calling can even become … a divine calling.

Truly, our work turns into our play as our play turns into our life. We become extremely genuine, much like children when left to exercise their minds by themselves with only their imagination for a mentor.

Our health and wellbeing tend to flourish when we live authentically. Stress lessens, endorphins increase, creativity soars, and our relationships (most importantly, with ourselves) deepen.

The personal power we gain from living in this type of alignment can't be overstated. Connecting with our true nature is a major treasure—one that just keeps giving—that we gain early on in the journey.

Authenticity (whatever that means on an individual basis) often opens doors to new interpersonal experiences and opportunities. Many people become magnets for like-minded individuals, building a community of support and inspiration. Others are empowered to embrace solitude and the inner voyage.

The more we get to know our authentic selves, the more we begin truly embodying our power. Living on our own terms is an act of defiance of the status quo that can forge us into energetic warriors in a shamanic sense, alchemists intent on powering up sufficiently to go *in* far enough to get *out* of here alive.

But even for those still attached to the Matrix, who can also benefit greatly from energy cultivation, undertaking the Hero's Journey to authenticity is a declaration that we're worthy of happiness and fulfillment.

This stance often translates to an earthly existence—the Dragon's efforts to sabotage us notwithstanding—filled with meaning and joy.

When we live *our* way, we invite others to do the same. We become beacons of hope and possibility. We create a quantum ripple effect encouraging those around us, near and far, to undertake their own heroic voyages of self-discovery.

To reiterate, the Hero's Journey isn't a destination, but an ongoing unfoldment. Our passions may evolve, our dreams may shift, and that's okay. When you're on the Hero's Journey of getting to know and becoming more and more of your total self, it's perfectly normal to wake up as a slightly different person each day.

Welcoming such developments—some of which can be unexpected, even dramatic—is key to living a life of continuous growth and fulfillment. As we learn and grow, we may discover new passions, we may feel called to follow our bliss in different directions.

This isn't a sign of failure, but a natural part of the unfolding of our multilayered identity. Like ourselves, our bliss is multidimensional and never static. It forever expands and changes alongside us.

Greet the unknown with openness, stay curious always, and never stop exploring as you become the best version of yourself—only to question that in turn before setting out in search of a newer and better best version.

CHAPTER FOURTEEN

Embrace Your Shadow

"No tree, it is said, can grow to heaven unless its roots reach down to hell."

—Carl Jung

Meet Your Shadow

Ever feel like there's a mysterious stranger at your own inner dinner party? You know, the one who spills wine on your best intentions, trips over the rug edge of your minutely laid plans, whispers doubts in your ear when the doorbell sounds?

That, my friend, is your shadow self waving hello from inside its cave and trying desperately to get your attention. Don't worry, especially in this book that already features a Dragon, a Ghost in the Machine and a Fragmentary Body, it's not nearly as spooky as it sounds.

Swiss psychiatrist and writer on inner alchemy Carl Jung called this hidden "problem child" within ourselves the shadow.

The shadow is the part of us that holds all the qualities we deem unacceptable, undesirable, or even downright embarrassing. Think of it as the dungeon of our psyche where we shove all the things we don't want to deal with or other people to see.

We're talking about our fears, insecurities, anger, selfishness, maybe even that secret crush on our brother's partner. It's like that seemingly bottomless junk drawer we all have—except instead of half-dead batteries and bent paperclips, the shadow overflows with repressed emotions and unacknowledged desires.

Now, you might be thinking, why on earth would I want to dig around in anyone's psychological dungeon, least of all my own?

Well, here's the thing. The shadow isn't inherently negative. It's just an aspect of ourselves that has been pushed far down into the darkness. Like a plant deprived of sunlight, it can grow in distorted and maladaptive ways if we don't acknowledge it.

"Everyone carries a shadow," explained Jung, "and the less it is embodied in the individual's conscious life, the blacker and denser it is. At all counts, it forms an unconscious snag, thwarting our most well-meant intentions."

Jung believed that the shadow, its problematic nature notwithstanding, holds immense power and potential for healing and transformation. By facing our shadow, we can begin reincorporating the suppressed aspects of ourselves with conscious awareness and access a greater sense of wholeness.

Imagine discovering a hidden room in your home filled with forgotten gold coins. That's sort of like the wealth of potential that lies within the cave of your shadow.

Embracing the shadow isn't about condoning or perpetuating negative behaviors. To the contrary, we're meant to understand their root in the shadow self so as to purify this toxic lead just weighing us down into pure gold that can lift us up.

Making Friends

The tricky thing about the shadow is that it practically never shows up sporting a name tag. Instead, we often project it onto others unknowingly. Like the proverbial forest we can't see for the trees, the shadow is often invisible while being right in front of our eyes.

Ever notice how quickly we judge other people for the very qualities we find disagreeable (even disgusting) in ourselves? That's the shadow hard at work showing you back to yourself. Masters of psychological projection, we point fingers, criticize, and judge—all the while remaining blissfully unaware of the same unacceptable traits lurking within us.

Denial is another pet stratagem of the shadow. We pretend those negative thoughts and impulses don't exist, burying them deeper and deeper inside. But just like that overstuffed suitcase we insist on cramming into the overhead compartment, our shadow inevitably pops open at the most wildly inconvenient times.

So how do we befriend this mysterious disruptive guest at our inner dinner party?

The first step is acknowledgment. Bring awareness to and admit your reactions to others. What pushes your buttons? What behaviors do you consider utter deal breakers? Chances are those are the very qualities you need to come to terms with in yourself.

Journaling, meditation and even beginner-level shamanic practices such as recapitulation (discussed in the next chapter) can be powerful tools for shadow work.

These practices can allow us to safely explore our inner landscape without fear or judgment while coaxing our shadow side back into the light of our awareness and acceptance.

Defining Shadow Work

"Shadow work" is a term we hear a lot these days, but what exactly does it *mean*?

First of all, shadow work is an internal process, usually a lengthy one. It's almost never a one-and-done silver bullet. It involves befriending all parts of ourselves, even the messy and cringe ones, while acknowledging our flaws and imperfections with compassion and understanding.

As we integrate our shadow, we shed layers upon layers of pretense while learning to be more genuine. We grow more accepting of ourselves and others, recognizing that we're all a mix of light and shadow, good and bad.

Performed consistently over time, shadow work has a way of becoming so empowering and fulfilling it actually transforms into … shadow play.

This development can be especially freeing with respect to the veritable *looshfest* that we find everywhere today but especially in religion and politics. Having integrated much of our shadow selves, we might still disagree with people voicing unsavory fundamentalist or politically charged opinions, but the situation no longer pulls our emotional strings.

This newfound sense of wholeness—particularly the psychological stability it provides—allows us to live with greater freedom and creativity, no longer bound by the inner chains of our unacknowledged selves being tugged on by outer circumstances.

Imagine a society where everyone embraced their shadows. Instead of blindly projecting our insecurities onto others, people would meet each other with open eyes, minds, and hearts. Conflicts would be resolved with greater ease and meaningful relationships would flourish almost effortlessly.

But it's not all beer and skittles. The journey of embracing our shadow definitely isn't for the faint of heart. You'll find no primrose path here.

It takes fortitude (and even attitude) to confront the parts of ourselves we've spent a lifetime avoiding. But the rewards can be monumental. By lighting up our darkness, we unlock the potential for profound growth and even outright transmutation of our "reality."

So the next time you feel triggered, irritated, flustered or judgmental, take a deep breath and ask yourself, *What part of me is the mirror of this moment reflecting?* It might just be your shadow knocking at the door, inviting you to embark on one of the most significant journeys of your life back to wholeness.

"Deep Shadow Work"

Going deeper still, shadow work means integrating not just the less desirable parts of our psyches—but even more importantly, using this as a springboard to holistically reclaim the totality of our subconscious and unconscious selves.

Crucially, this self-reclamation project involves getting to know and work with the shadow behind your shadow, the Ghost in the Machine, your magical "brain child" illuminating your Hero's Journey into the Dark Sea of Awareness.

In *The Way of the Projectionist* John Kreiter describes the Ghost as the fortuitous product of the rebellion of the unconscious when suppressed by the installation of the Dragon's operating system, the terribly misunderstood and misnamed conscious mind.

Whether the Ghost emerged by accident or some hidden design is open to debate. Whatever the case, harmonizing with the Ghost allows us to awaken it within ourselves and, with its necessary assistance, begin the metamorphic process of uniting our conscious and unconscious minds so as to heal our internal duality that keeps us separated from ourselves.

This "deep shadow work," if you will, is only accessed by paying less and less of our precious attention to the Matrix as we go far, far *inward* in order to open the door infinitely *outward* to the Undiscovered Country beyond.

Engaging in deep shadow work provides us with the means of pursuing further integration of our totality with the potential to create an immortal identity.

Two Sides of Trauma

Shadow work, in all its forms, further entails getting real about the nature of our relationship to the Dragon. To reiterate a crucial point, a nearly always overlooked plot element in the human story is this: during the Dreamtime of our prehistory, we ourselves, desiring to be more than we were, dreamed our spiritual adversary into existence.

Now it's up to us, individually and perhaps collectively, if we wish to make yet another quantum leap in our beingness, to dream the Dragon out of existence—or at the very least change our relationship to it in the here and now.

Trauma in an absurdly profound predicament such as ours can be a blockage to the full expression of our authentic selves, energetically speaking. That said, trauma can also be an invitation to transcend and go beyond the limitations of the Matrix.

Think of trauma, then, as a double-edged sword. All the triggers, aggressions and microaggressions being thrown at us by the Dragon in this spiritual dojo—however potentially insulting, damaging and even tragic they might be—are also invitations to "aikido" them, deflect them, use that energy for ourselves.

It's absolutely possible to do this. I'm not saying it's a piece of cake. But if you stick with me through the end of this book, I promise to give you a roadmap for exactly how to start doing it.

Spirits on a Journey beyond This World

In the meantime allow me to point out that we're dancing around the essence of martial arts here. I'm not just speaking philosophically—but literally about using negative energy for one's own spiritual growth and energetic empowerment.

I mean that we can purposely, actually, like an aikido master, take the Dragon's ill-begotten energy and turn away only to empower ourselves with it.

In other words, as mentioned, we can reverse the entire *loosh* dynamic here in this construct by learning to prey on the apex predator's stolen energy!

We're here for a reason, don't let anyone tell you otherwise. Our trials and tribulations are meant to awaken us to the vastness of our genuine nature and potential as souls on a journey of human learning … and beyond.

The unpacking of our innate ability to transcend any and all limitations involves the cultivation of power, regardless of how you go about it. Personal power is the gateway to exiting the World Cult, getting out of the Matrix. And with the possible exception of the earth itself, the single greatest source of power there is in this realm is—you guessed it—the Dragon.

Like it or not, fume and pout as much as your victimhood allows (if this describes you), but a central motif here is that we're in a spiritual classroom. The English poet John Keats perhaps characterized this world best as a "Vale of Soul-making."

In this radically elucidating perspective, we actually don't come here *as* souls, old or new. Rather, our souls are forged *here*, in real time, in this alchemical crucible of a world.

It's as if, after splintering off from the totality of our God-self, we must first become individual spirits. As such we pursue individuation and reintegration of the totality of our divine nature … before we get bored, I suppose, with unity and eternity and … do it all again …

Yes, we're back to the ouroboros and its never-ending loop. If you haven't done so already, note the shape of the image at the end of each chapter in this book. It's an infinity sign.

If you ask me, this dreamlike existence is obviously a kind of test preparing us for … some kind of matriculation out of the Matrix. Observe that the root of both "matriculation" and "Matrix" refers to the womb.

In my humble opinion, it couldn't be more blatantly coded into the construct that our graduation from this school of hard knocks is designed to culminate in a bio-spiritual birth, or rebirth.

Our challenge is the privilege of learning to conflate with our own greatness as we say sayonara to this distracting funhouse, energized by the Dragon's own bon voyage gift of power—however unwillingly given.

Reclaiming our totality probably wouldn't be a simple task under any circumstances. But it's especially difficult on a Gameboard designed to keep people looking outside instead of in.

Before I got a lot older and a little wiser, I used to think the current generation of "truthers" were much deeper thinkers than most of them have shown themselves to be.

There tends to be a lot of smoke around their words, I've observed, but very little fire of awareness. I keep waiting for more of them to figure out that they're playing a game that's rigged against them.

Most of them don't (and may never) realize that the only way they can win is to *stop playing*. As in the much-shared but only superficially interpreted meme from the classic movie *WarGames*, "The only winning move is not to play."

And the most powerful—if not, strictly speaking, only—way not to play is to go from the *outside* to the *inside*. Be willing to do the inner, the shadow work. Put on your big boy or big girl pants and set out on the absurdly profound journey of transforming yourself, truly and lastingly, into all you can be.

In the grand scheme of your spiritual evolution, whatever might be going on in the external world, as distracting as it may be, simply doesn't matter. Even worse, it's likely to serve as a sneaky impediment to your becoming.

In the spiritual realm, distraction (focusing on the outside) leads to inaction (not going inside). Or to put it in terms you might have heard elsewhere, *analysis leads to paralysis*.

However we phrase this situation, it's a recipe for a slow disaster of stasis, unfulfilled potential, and eventual death and loss of your unique individual consciousness as your memories and awareness are swallowed by the Great Dark Sea.

In this vision of "heaven," you're destined to meet your maker, all right. But instead of doing this as equals, you'll have completely forgotten who you were as what makes you you is utterly and irrevocably reabsorbed back into the One Consciousness.

For the record I'm *not* saying bad things aren't happening in the so-called real world "out there." I get it. This isn't my first rodeo. Shit happens. It happened to me. It will probably happen again. Such is life.

But I *am* saying that you really don't have much control over anything except yourself. Get used to it.

And use this starkly honest perspective to jump-start your sense of personal responsibility for your ultimate fate as you undertake the Hero's Journey into your cave and begin working together with all the many aspects of your shadow ... and its shadow in turn.

"I See Myself in You"

"Engagé," from the French, is an adjective describing someone passionately committed to a "real-world" cause. Prior to grasping the nature of this *loosh* farm, how it's actually a World Cult designed for trafficking the power of human attention, I used to be very *engagé* myself.

This was especially the case during the orchestrated pandemic whose seeds were sown by the Dragon and its minions to insure a historic energy harvest. Even in its aftermath, they're still milking every last drop of *loosh* from this intentional traumatizing of the world.

But then, after engaging in some serious self-reflection, I was forced to swallow a bitter pill myself. I saw very clearly what actually motivates activists—especially the ones who haven't done their inner and shadow work.

When we throw ourselves body, mind and soul into activism (whether it's saving the planet, protecting the environment, or any other externally focused militancy), we're actually engaging in fear-based, Dragon-driven *narcissism*.

We may tell ourselves—and anyone who cares to listen— otherwise. We may pretend to be doing "God's work" or the "right thing" as we "fight the good fight" ... "against all enemies, foreign and domestic" ... "for our children." And we might even believe our own lies.

Some activists might also be inclined to come down on you hard for expressing your reservations and not jumping on the bandwagon of their pet cause. They might even use shaming or other tactics to stealthily recruit you into some aspect of the Dragon's divide-and-conquer game of distractions.

That such activists (who are almost always, when it boils right down to it, more *against* than *for* things) are ultimately coming from a place of fear, not altruism, should be apparent.

And since they're afraid, not only are they leaking *loosh*; they're also easily manipulated via their foreign operating system, the Dragon's mimetic mind.

But really, just as with the illusory nature of matter we touched on in Chapter 1, there's simply no real there there when it comes to psychically projected "opponents" or "enemies."

When I published my first book, *Conscious Healing*, seemingly a lifetime ago in the mid-aughts, I shared many thoughts on unity consciousness, the idea that we're all one. I hear people giving this concept lip service constantly, but rarely do I find them following it through to its absurdly profound conclusion.

Me, I take the idea of unity consciousness where it (il)logically leads. If we're all one, this means there's one—and *only* one—consciousness here. Ergo, appearances notwithstanding, *we're having an illusory experience of separation*.

The multidimensional Dark Sea surrounding and encompassing our little corner of "reality" is actually one gigantic being. We're part of that being experiencing itself as … ourselves. Through a particular application of creative attention, we've falsely convinced ourselves that we're divided from the divine spark that gave us our sense of self.

But if you trace the totality of yourself all the way back to your origin in the field of being, you must inevitably conclude that you're just … God. Technically, rather than "star stuff," to use a phrase made famous by Carl Sagan, we're "God stuff."

"When I speak of imagination I am referring to God in you," said Neville Goddard. He also specified, with vast implications relative to our discussion of reclaiming the totality of ourselves by uniting with the immense creative power of our unconscious mind, "The dreamer in you is God."

At the risk of oversimplification, we're God dreaming or imagining that we're not—while suffering the consequences and reaping the rewards of our divinely instigated experiences—until we learn to consciously acknowledge our true pandimensional nature.

What exactly happens at that moment is anybody's guess. But at this point, we can at least affirm that illusion of otherness is an integral aspect of this classroom. It means that we're also, that we can *only* be, fundamentally, our own adversary as well.

The shadows on the walls of our cave are just … ourselves. We're the Dragon because … *we're all each other*.

In my novel *Snooze: A Story of Awakening* about harnessing the power of attention to do the impossible by mastering the second world of dreams, the characters my protagonist meets in this Undiscovered Country living on the Shores of the Dark Sea of Awareness, as it were, greet each other by saying, "I see myself in you."

Consider the profoundly absurd implications for a second. This isn't just a spin on *Avatar* where the Na'vi say "I see you" to indicate respectful connection with the other.

Seeing yourself in someone else is about collapsing the boundaries between self and other. To once again cite the popular aphorism I think I first heard Ram Dass use, *there's only one of us here*.

If everyone thought that way, what a shockingly different Matrix we'd be inhabiting!

Thesis, Antithesis, Synthesis

"Truthers" tend to believe in getting to the bottom of objective facts, generating real solutions, solving material problems, making things physically better on a large scale.

Of course, none of these outcomes will likely ever happen—certainly not on the central stage of the malleable Matrix that is the World Cult.

Most of the population would scoff at the idea that we're living in a fictional construct. One could include "truthers" in this majority, even though they often intellectually grasp the idea of "reality" as a kind of *Tron*-like Gameboard.

A much smaller group of shamans, inner alchemists and other explorers of consciousness are actively endeavoring to exit the Matrix itself. These are the ones who truly interest me, the "mad ones, the ones who are mad to live," as Jack Kerouac might have described them. Maybe you're one of them.

Meanwhile, blindly going *out* instead of looking *in*, "truthers" are controlled by their controllers. The latter are the elite minions of the Dragon who make sure that not just the mainstream but the alternative media as well spin their dystopian narratives in order to bring them about.

It's not so much that these high-up controllers are spellcasters (a common meme in conspiracy circles). Instead, it's more the case that they're gifted at directing society's discourse makers to parasitize people's most valuable ability, the one that allows them to create reality through their own narratives about it. We ourselves, then, are the real spellcasters in this equation.

"Truthers," as mentioned, are controlled opposition, knowingly or otherwise. Indeed, as a meme I recently shared beautifully phrased it, *All opposition is controlled opposition.*

Long-term focus on the negative isn't without its own negative consequences either. To paraphrase Friedrich Nietzsche, truthers who stare too long into the darkness turn into the monsters they observe.

This shot of tough love enrages a lot of people, especially "truthers." And yet an endless number of doomsday scenarios are being pushed forward and galvanized by just such witting and unwitting supporters of the Dragon's hive-mind agenda.

To think that "truthers" are fundamentally different from the mainstream media is ludicrous. They're yin and yang, two sides of the same coin used by the Duality Cult to bifurcate minds and people into an ultimate synthesis of control.

Thesis, antithesis, synthesis. This is the dialectical model of mind control happening in the here and now, for anyone willing to remove their blindfold, and yet so few are willing to see it.

Are you ready to open your eyes and plot your course to freedom? In order to make this happen, are you prepared to embrace your shadow and your shadow's shadow, something today's busy "truthers" seem categorically unwilling to spend time doing?

Are you ready to begin recovering your lost energy and building up your personal power in order to heal and move forward on your Hero's Journey here in this world, certainly, and perhaps even out into the Great Unknown?

CHAPTER FIFTEEN

Recover Lost Energy & Heal Trauma with Shamanic Recapitulation

"[R]ecapitulation ... consisted of a systematic scrutiny of one's life, segment by segment, an examination made not in the light of criticism or finding flaw, but in the light of an effort to understand one's life, and to change its course. Don Juan's claim was that once any practitioner has viewed his life in the detached manner that the recapitulation requires, there's no way to go back to the same life." —Carlos Castaneda

Dipping Your Toe in the Dark Sea of Awareness

There are many methods offered by various schools and individual practitioners of shamanism to "recapitulate" your life. The majority of these techniques—which are usually but not always rather similar—tend to be effective in helping to address trauma and recover squandered energy.

The one I'll teach you how to do momentarily is based on the style of recapitulation associated with Toltec shamanism and made famous in the misjudged and often maliciously maligned works of Carlos Castaneda.

In these controversial books that have been translated into numerous languages and sold millions of copies, the author claims that recapitulation and other techniques for cultivating power were taught to him by his teacher, the enigmatic Don Juan Matus, who was allegedly drawing on a long tradition of shamanism reaching back many generations.

The confusing morass of mystery surrounding Castaneda and his books (fiction? nonfiction? fantasy? memoir?) is, in my humble opinion, just another absurdly profound proof of the unavailability of … definitive proof in this construct.

Be that as it may, recapitulation is considered by many a foundational technique for increasing one's store of energy. It's also a strict requirement for anybody on one of the shamanic paths said to have originated in Mesoamerica. Having benefited from it greatly myself, I can't praise it enough.

I consider recapitulation an excellent starting point for anyone interested in testing the waters of the Dark Sea of Awareness. Recapitulation allows you to explore the inner reaches of your consciousness in a safe and controlled manner—often with undeniable, even tangible mind-body-spirit benefits.

This method of increasing personal power by lessening and sometimes healing old energetic wounds and resultant traumas seems to work best when you're simultaneously intent on simplifying your life and pulling back from situations and connections that drain your energy, as covered in previous chapters.

But even people on the go, go, go can benefit from this work—so long as they're able to regularly carve out even a little bit of time from the whirlwind of their busy-ness.

Thoroughly detailed by Castaneda's cohort Taisha Abelar in *The Sorcerer's Crossing*, recapitulation is described as having been traditionally carried out in caves, a hole in the ground, an empty grave, or even a coffin (box) of one's own fabrication that was ceremonially immolated upon completion of this protracted exercise.

Yes, recapitulating your life story, which can go on for months or even years, isn't a quick fix. But embraced as an ongoing wellness practice, it can lead to both short-term results and long-term transformation.

Other (particularly younger) shamans—including another of Castaneda's colleagues, who shared her experience of a life-changing recapitulation she performed while squeezed into a packed Mexican bus—have softened the older, more stringent requirements for this practice.

Nowadays people recapitulate their lives in a dark closet, or seated in an armchair with eyes closed, or even lying in bed. Personally, I prefer the latter venue, complete with a sleep mask and earplugs to shut out the world while remaining comfortable and relaxed.

The Basic Technique

The Toltec version of recapitulation employs a rhythmic and soothing technique typically known as the "fan breath."

Begin with your head positioned facing either side. As your head slowly rotates to the opposite side, roughly one hundred and eighty degrees (or as far as your flexibility comfortably allows), focus on any memory containing residual energy or unresolved trauma.

Feel free to do this with random memories that just pop into your thoughts (a "right-brain" approach). Alternatively, you can choose to list the specific memories you want to address in more of a "left-brain" fashion. Some people write them down, others go from memory.

You can progress through your whole life in order, starting even as far back as your gestation or even conception (which you'll just have to imagine). Or you can go in reverse order through your personal timeline back to your stint in the womb or moment of conception.

However you opt to proceed (and don't be afraid to alter your approach and experiment), *breathe in* through the nose any power or parts of yourself you left behind in that episode from your past.

Then, while rotating your head slowly back to its initial sideways position, *breathe out* (again, through the nose) any and all energy fragments that might have been taken (knowingly or otherwise) from others (living or dead) that belong to them.

It can be helpful to visualize this energy as brightly colored bands or ribbons as it returns to you, and black-and-white bands or ribbons as it leaves you and goes back to its rightful owner(s).

Processing through all your charged and important memories, either in chronological order or by skipping around to whatever's calling your attention, is a highly involved undertaking.

As you can probably imagine, it can last many months (at a minimum), over the course of which you may need to revisit certain memories and associated traumas multiple times.

While the practice requires a considerable amount of dedication, I can assure you it's absolutely worth your patience and effort.

An Alternative Form of Recapitulation

Quetzaltzin ("Venerable Quetzal"), which comes from the Tol (not to be confused with Toltec) lineage of Mesoamerican shamanism, has in recent years been popularized by author Sergio Magaña as an alternative way of performing recapitulation.

As described in *The Toltec Secret*, this "Different Venerable and Accounts of Our Life" is done wearing *xayaca*, or special masks, while reciting your life story in front of a mirror for at least half an hour every day for thirty-six consecutive days.

Magaña claims that as "time goes by, the story of your life and your own face become detached from each other until the link is broken completely. Once that relationship is over, the story of your life will stop affecting you."

This remarkable result is absolutely consistent with those of many similar shamanic techniques found in Castaneda's writings employed to "erase personal history" and "stalk the self" into greater awareness of one's own amazing multiplicity in order to achieve more and more freedom from the Matrix.

Quetzaltzin also, over time, is said to increase lucidity, particularly in dreams, eventually giving way to what Magaña calls the "blossom dream." In such a lucid dream, it's said that fresh seeds of possibility can be planted to power up one's life to flower in unprecedented ways.

Personally, after considerable experience with both approaches, I prefer Castaneda and Abelar's version of recapitulation.

While using masks is a fascinating psychological exercise with its own set of unique benefits in terms of shaping a new consciousness, in my opinion the fan breath is more effective in undoing trauma and restoring energy in palpable and immediately useful ways.

That said, I encourage you to listen to your own intuition and instincts. By all means, do whatever works for you. We're all different expressions of the One Consciousness— and thank goodness!

Empower Yourself to Heal Your World

If you decide to go with the fan breath approach, here are some additional thoughts and considerations to help you better innerstand what you're doing and maximize your results.

By performing half-hour (give or take) recapitulation sessions two or three times per week, preferably early in the day so as not to rev up your system just before bedtime, a couple of transformational dynamics eventually come into play.

First, you're fast-tracking your reacquisition of personal power. This can potentially produce any number of benefits, including greater get-up-and-go, more sex drive, improved mood, deeper sleep, better relationships, and even resolution of chronic health issues.

Be on the lookout for these kinds of developments, or even ones of a similar but comparatively minor nature that indicate that your energy levels are most definitely trending upward.

Even as you take back your own power, you're simultaneously giving back vital energy you accidentally or otherwise took from other significant characters in your life story.

This can include friends, enemies, lovers, teachers, parents, bosses, colleagues, and seemingly random individuals who influenced your trajectory through cameo appearances.

This reclaiming of our own while giving back others' power can have truly miraculous effects.

In my particular case, I was recapitulating a close relative with whom I had unresolved interpersonal issues. I was processing my memories of him when he experienced a major breakthrough in his mental health even as our relationship suddenly improved, drastically, for no other obvious reason.

So dramatic was this change that my relative, who also had an interest in shamanism, came out and asked me point-blank if I'd been recapitulating our relationship! When I admitted that I had been, he shared his transformational experience of being on the receiving end of *my* process!

As in the previously referenced adage, through recapitulation you truly are healing the world (or at least *your* world) as you heal yourself.

The critical thing is that you recapitulate until you've reclaimed as much of your personal energy as you can and given back every last shred of energy that didn't belong to you to start with.

Well before this stage, you'll probably begin observing a variety of unambiguous changes in such areas as self-talk, general outlook, overall mood, lifestyle, and even personality.

At some point you may sense that you've accomplished your personal healing goals and you'll put recapitulation behind you as you move on with your life in the Matrix with renewed power and purpose.

But sooner or later, you also may have things you'd like to work on or achieve. Maybe you're still not altogether satisfied with your energy and empowerment levels. Or perhaps your foray into shamanism has made you wonder if there are even more transformational strategies than recapitulation.

That's how you'll know that your internal hero is calling you to consider an even deeper journey into the depths of yourself through inner alchemy.

CHAPTER SIXTEEN

Create Your Own Philosopher's Stone through Inner Alchemy

"The secrets of alchemy exist to transform mortals from a state of suffering and ignorance to a state of enlightenment and bliss." —Deepak Chopra

Healing & Regenerating Your Multidimensional Self

If recapitulation is like breaking the sound barrier in terms of reaccumulating energy by tidying up one's wasteful past, inner alchemy as described in *The Magnum Opus* trilogy of books by John Kreiter is like hitting warp drive and traveling faster than light.

Indeed, this absurdly profound methodology—which explicitly envisages time and the discrete self as both merely illusions—not only allows you to travel into your "past" (which encompasses endless alternative versions thereof) for healing, trauma resolution, and revitalization.

Using a somewhat nuanced version of the energy reabsorption technique Kreiter shares (which I'll outline shortly), you can even undertake a Hero's Journey into any number of possible "futures" and restore energy and wellbeing you've inadvertently "paid forward" through negative forms of creative attention such as fear, worry, and stress.

Think of this process as healing and regenerating your multidimensional self—the totality that we might call the Dark Sea of Possibilities that is the true you—along multiple timelines stretching both "forward" and "backward" in the purely fictitious construct known as time.

Alchemy Isn't What You Think

Perhaps you've studied alchemy or read a little about it—in which case you likely have an image of crusty curmudgeons performing arcane "chemistry" experiments in an attempt to turn lead into gold and create the immortality-granting Philosopher's Stone.

Countless books and movies—including the first installment of *Harry Potter* and, more recently, *A Discovery of Witches*—have hammered home such a caricatural version of alchemy.

But let's be totally honest: many alchemists themselves, genuine and spurious, haven't done the discipline any favors either.

Abstruse and often arcanely illustrated tomes bizarrely mixing scientific elements with poetic flights of fancy and even bold-faced fantasy line the dusty library shelves of European history.

Seemingly penned inside asylums, the profusion of confusing and downright dodgy alchemical works has led contemporary scientists—smugly confident that their newfangled methods myopically rooted in reason have cornered the market on truth—to dismiss alchemy as equal parts superstition and hooey.

Here's the thing, though. It's true that many fledgling alchemists literally had no idea what they were talking about and actually thought alchemy was primarily concerned with manipulating matter.

It can be used that way, yes, but only if done *in the right order*. Focusing on manipulation of the so-called material world in the first instance is to put the cart before the horse and end up going nowhere.

Authentic medieval, Renaissance and even later alchemists, on the other hand, knowing that teaching effective alchemical techniques to the uninitiated would only serve to bring the inquisitorial wrath of the Church down on their heads, were inclined to communicate in code.

One such alchemist was the Englishman George Ripley, whose work influenced John Dee, Robert Boyle (considered the first chemist), and even Isaac Newton. Ripley's esoteric knowledge may have been referenced by an anonymous author in a document known as *The Ripley Scroll*.

A particularly relevant and accurate stanza, alchemically speaking, from this occult treatise states:

Thou must part him in three
And then knit him as the Trinity
And make them all but one
Lo here is the Philosophers Stone

The author of the scroll is clearly (if cleverly) referring to the Tria Prima, the triune alchemical "recipe" that focuses on energetically uniting the three polarities that combine to grant us access to the totality of ourselves.

In the top layer of the code designed to hide alchemy's real treasures of inner transformation under a veneer of pseudo-chemistry, the Tria Prima appears to be referencing sulfur, salt, and mercury.

But for the initiated, these elements secretly corresponded to the Father (the primal unconscious self), the Son (the Dragon's mental installation, or conscious mind, once set to rights by the Father), and the Holy Spirit (the exalted form of the Ghost in the Machine, that part of our total psyche that unites the Father and Son).

Importantly, Kreiter points out that the Tria Prima recipe also indicates the threefold dynamic of projecting one's attention *in* in order to get *out* of the Matrix while utilizing the Ghost's ability to mediate between these dualistic modalities by way of the *void* state of awareness.

In short, contrary to popular opinion, genuine alchemy isn't directly about manipulating the "material world" at all. Rather, it's a time-tested discipline for amassing personal energy and, simultaneously, honing the immense power of our creative attention to go far, far beyond the world we know.

Alchemy's ultimate goal, it goes almost without saying, doesn't involve creating a shiny rock you can hold in your hand that lets you live forever. If you think about it for a moment, that's just plain silly.

Instead, its aim is to empower the individual practitioner to cultivate, over time, an energetic powerhouse—called the Philosopher's Stone—within his or her own body, thus granting oneself a chance to become eternal.

Other Possible Avenues for Cheating Death

The Philosopher's Stone is a stepping stone to real immortality, and alchemy is at least one way of creating it. There may be, however, other ways of doing so or of becoming immortal in a different fashion.

In two of my previous books, I examined a number of interrelated esoteric phenomena that sometimes figure in discussions of immortality.

In *Conscious Healing* I did a deep dive into what has been called the lightbody, a.k.a. the Rainbow Body. I proposed that it might be achievable through "ener-genetic" stimulation leading to a "transposition burst" in which DNA suddenly mutates to create a new life form … in a single generation.

Other names for the lightbody, I noted, include Diamond Body and Jade Body (Taoism), Glorified Body (Christianity), Holy Flesh (Catholicism), Merkabah (Kabala), Adamantine Body (Tantra), Superconductive Body (Vedanta), Supercelestial Body (Sufism), Radiant Body (Neo-Platonism), Body of Bliss (Kriya Yoga), Perfect Body (Mithraism), and Immortal Body (Hermeticism).

Following up on this exceedingly thought-provoking material, in *The World Cult & You* I looked at what Carlos Castaneda referred to as the "Fire from Within" in his book by the same title.

The Fire from Within refers to the alleged ability of shamans who have gathered enough power—via recapitulation and other techniques—to die while maintaining their consciousness intact … only to reconfigure themselves in the Dark Sea of Awareness and voyage on into eternity.

I pointed out that in Sergio Magaña's introduction of a parallel shamanic lineage, there was also a similar possibility of achieving transcendence. The "ultimate purpose of nahualism," he explains, is "finally, rather than dying, to become fire, like a Queztalcóatl."

I further called attention to parallels to the Fire from Within in the East, where Tibetan master Chögyal Namkhia Noru focuses on lucid dreaming and related practices in Dzogchen that—like those of Toltec shamanism—supposedly allow for an alternative way to die in which self-awareness is preserved.

As you can see, beginning with that simple question in front of Jim Morrison's grave, I've spent decades contemplating the "problem" of mortality.

Imagine my delight and excitement when I discovered Kreiter's work and began experimenting with, and eventually personalizing, the working concepts he shares—which I'm pleased to say are indeed exceedingly powerful.

"Ghosting" Yourself

Without further ado let's start getting into the nitty-gritty of how to go about generating your very own Philosopher's Stone. While occasionally adding my own touch or insights, I'll be synthesizing the most important aspects of the basic technique that Kreiter covers.

In *The Magnum Opus* we're given to understand that this straightforward method, as Kreiter presents it stripped of metaphor and arcane symbols, has been employed by inner alchemists for generations. In a sense, then, I'm simply passing along to you the gist of what was passed along to Kreiter before me. To be absolutely clear, I'm not in any way affiliated with him and he hasn't endorsed this book.

I recommend that you use this chapter as a springboard for further research into this topic and technique. If inner alchemy truly interests you, you'll eventually want to read the other two works in Kreiter's trilogy that go into much greater detail on this subject of subjects: *The Way of the Projectionist* and *The Way of the Death Defier*.

As mentioned in the Preface, you may also benefit from PragmAlchemy, my series of original practices for enhancing your work in practical inner alchemy available at **solluckman.substack.com**.

In order to begin creating your Philosopher's Stone, the first thing to do is to learn to activate your "energy pumps." These are aspects of your Ghost in the Machine, your magical mutant, the "Luminous Child" that's your #1 ally in undoing the Dragon's control over your mind and helping you get the heck out of here alive.

Technically, as in igniting the Fire from Within, your exit from the Matrix requires relinquishing the physical body that you know and stepping into a completely new body— which I've sometimes called the Dreambody with reference to the late great Arnold Mindell's classic book of the same title.

From the perspective of inner alchemy, while maintaining your own memories and personality, in making this transition you're actually conflating with your Ghost as it turns into your Holy Ghost.

This greatly expanded arrangement (which Kreiter calls the Unitary Entity, a.k.a. the Phoenix) becomes your new multidimensional body for navigating infinity as you fly over the waters of eternity all the way back, eventually, to full Source consciousness.

Your new immortal body made for the second world is far more capable of experiencing the sometimes nuanced and chaotic realms that make up the Dark Sea of Awareness. And by all accounts, it's also a lot more exciting to be in than the extremely limited physical body!

If you've ever had a dream that seemed so real you could taste it, or so sexy you could feel it, or so touching you woke up in tears, or so riveting it gave you goosebumps, or so electrifying you came to gasping, then you've glimpsed the kind of hyper-realistic experience that's in store for you in your new and improved form.

Pump It Up

To activate your energy pumps, start by pretending to employ telekinesis to move a small object toward you. Say, a pencil. (If you're a member of a younger generation who doesn't know what that is, try moving your smartphone instead.)

The goal isn't to levitate the pencil (or smartphone) with the pittance of energy currently available to you after a lifetime of being *looshed*. What you're after is to identify the *feeling* of activating your sleepy inner Ghost to simply make the attempt to move the object.

When this occurs, you're likely to sense energetic movement originating in or around your navel area (the lower *dantian* in tai chi and qigong) and extending outward to the object in an attempt to "grab" it and "pull" it toward you.

This is significant because in Chinese martial arts as well as in shamanism and inner alchemy, the solar plexus region is the seat of personal power.

This area is also related to the Fragmentary Body, a critically important subject for those pursuing deep levels of healing and transformation which I'll unpack further in the next chapter.

If you're a male, it's here just behind your belly button in this spherical area roughly the size of a tennis ball Kreiter calls the "Cauldron" that you'll be storing the energy that you absorb (and reabsorb) and refine. And it's here in your Cauldron that you'll eventually create and house your Philosopher's Stone.

But note that in alchemy, men and women aren't created equal. In fact, females are far more capable alchemists. This is the case because they can use their entire uterine area—not just the small Cauldron available to men—to store power.

If you're a woman reading this, when I speak of the Cauldron, be sure to visualize the full region of your womb. This applies even if you no longer have one, as this area will maintain its etheric functionality to house hyperdimensional energy.

For men Kreiter recommends using your inner feeling sense—your intuition combined with your imagination, roughly—to determine the exact location of your Cauldron, since it can be slightly higher or lower than the navel.

But if you have any trouble identifying it initially, don't worry. Just intuit and imagine where it is and start the energy gathering process in good faith.

Over time, if you're like me, you'll probably begin to feel this area more and more as it powers up. Based on my experience, you may also, especially in the beginning, sense it moving ever so slightly—up or down, left or right, forward or backward, or even a combination. This, too, appears to be normal.

Once you've become good at feeling yourself *pull* your pencil or smartphone toward you, try the opposite maneuver and attempt to *push* it away.

As before, it's really your Ghost that's doing the pushing, which manifests as a subtle force you should sense likewise originating in the general area of your Cauldron or womb.

As soon as you're comfortable pushing and pulling with your energy pumps, you're in a position to begin reabsorbing your lost energy in the past and even the future. But first, to get our alchemical sea legs on for our adventures in time travel, let's practice absorbing natural energy in the here and now.

Energy Absorption

Start small with, say, a wild or house plant. Using your inner feeling sense, you should be able to connect (at least conceptually at the outset) with its energy that, like your own aura, it automatically projects into the environment.

Stand or sit in front of the plant and, with your tongue pressed against the hard palate in your mouth just behind your upper front teeth and using the pulling action of your Ghost's energy pumps, imagine drawing some of the plant's energy into you.

Practice doing this with your hands first. Then repeat the process with your feet, then your shoulder blades, then your skull, and finally your whole body including your skin and bones.

Don't be concerned that you'll hurt the plant. Our vegetal friends appear far more resilient than people in this respect. If you feel that you've taken all the energy you should but you're still wanting to practice, simply thank the first plant for its help and move to a second one.

Pressing the tongue against the roof of the mouth whenever you're absorbing or reabsorbing energy is extremely important. This is because it completes one of the body's central energy pathways referred to as the "microcosmic orbit."

The exact position of the tongue doesn't matter so much, as long as it's pressed firmly but comfortably against the hard palate. Look up a diagram of the mouth online or in a reference book if you're fuzzy as to the precise layout of this part of your anatomy.

By maintaining proper tongue position, you keep the energy you're pulling in from pooling or stagnating in your system, which can lead to irritation, inflammation, pain, and even healing crises (Herxheimer reactions).

Regardless of which body part you're using to *pull* through, the energy will quickly make its way to a point I like to call your "intake valve" between your shoulder blades and, from there, descend into your stomach.

You might feel a tingling in your arms or legs. That's completely natural. I sometimes experience an almost imperceptible (and usually short-lived) "itching" sensation on my skin. That appears normal, too.

Once the energy has made its way into your stomach, using this organ's largely unacknowledged secondary function as an energy purifier, your Ghost refines or distills the raw "food" you've sucked in by thoroughly "digesting" it.

In order to make this food truly your own and ready for your own use, without impurities or any bad or dirty energy from its source, be sure to adopt—mentally and emotionally—a "Predatory Stance" as you ingest your energetic "prey."

Pretend you're a lion, for example, feasting on a fresh kill. Nobody in his or her right mind would dare to come near you until you're finished with the carcass. Feel how this energy is now *yours* and *nothing*, not even the Dragon, can take it from you if you don't want it to.

It's "very important that you take on a Predatory Stance," Kreiter emphasizes, "because in this way you void negative intention and superimpose your own positive intent upon it."

Keep thinking like a feeding predator for several minutes as you connect with your Ghost and digest your newly acquired energy. I like to imagine that the energy starts out as a swirling, milky cloud that my stomach slowly purifies until it's like liquified gold.

When the energy feels good and refined, it's time to place it in your Cauldron. Do this by once again activating your Ghost's pumping capability.

At this point you have two options. You can either *push* the now golden energy from your stomach down into your Cauldron, or you can *pull* it down from your stomach for storage.

Once every last potent drop of the energy is relocated, having refined it properly, you're now ready to store it using a process called *packing*. This is the stage where you begin transforming your absorbed energy into what will gradually become your Philosopher's Stone.

Activating your energy pumps yet again, imagine pushing and pulling the energy into a compact little ball, the tighter and smaller the better. Visualize the ball glowing brighter and brighter as you condense it. Mine appears bright red like molten lava.

A few minutes spent packing should suffice for smaller energy helpings; larger amounts of power require longer stints. I tend to keep my tongue against my palate even at this stage, since it's not a bad idea to maintain one's full-body meridian circuit throughout this entire process.

Packing—while working with subtle energy instead of material substance—is comparable to adding pressure to coal to slowly turn it into a diamond.

After quite a few months spent processing mother lodes of raw energy, you may begin to sense the Philosopher's Stone as a sort of quasi liquid crystal, something multidimensional but slowly becoming more "solid," a "piezoelectric gem" in incipient form whose final completion will take years.

Meanwhile, enjoy the many and varied benefits—which can include everything from better health and wellness to increased cognitive capacity and attention span—that boosting your personal power in this fashion typically brings.

Going to the Next Level with People Power

After you've practiced on small plants for a bit, feel free to up your game by switching to trees and even whole forests. Eventually, you'll feel that you're ready to begin harvesting even more intense energy in the human realm from unpleasant and negative interactions involving other people.

Note that I'm *not* suggesting that you experiment with vampirism by feeding on your fellow human beings. But interpersonal interactions can and often do generate *loosh* on one or both sides of an undesirable situation, and *loosh* is fair game because it no longer belongs to anyone in particular.

Your prize in this exercise is the energy that has already been flushed out of people and is headed straight into the Dragon's mouth anyway.

This energy is now lost to the unfortunate soul from whom it was extracted, and you're simply finding and making good use of it. As the sports saying goes, no harm, no foul.

"It is imperative that you always push beyond [your] fear and timidity," counsels Kreiter when addressing some people's reservations relative to energy absorption. He continues:

> EAT THIS TIMIDITY like you have consumed all the other silly emotional drains of your day. And then use this consumed fear and timidity to push out the strong being that resides within you, a being strong enough to feed on those negativities and those harmful beings that would bring you down, cause you harm, or even feed on your energy.

Begin by absorbing your own energy flares. The next time you experience anger, fear or another unpleasant emotion that would normally drain you, pretend you're your own house plant as you absorb your own ambient energy (or more accurately in this case, *loosh* on the loose).

Be sure to *stay as relaxed as possible* throughout (re)absorbing, refining and storing the *loosh* waves pulsing through and beyond the frequency bands of your personal aura.

Relaxation makes the whole process of pulling in power much easier, more enjoyable, and less subject to headaches and other aches and pains that can result from a spike in tension as energy is added to your circuits.

To take the next step in mastering the absorption technique, you might consider starting out in the comfort and safety of your own home by watching the evening news (*only* for this exercise and never, *ever* again—if you value your mental health).

Wait for a story about something tragic (you won't have to wait long), identify one of its living victims, and try to feel the *loosh* flowing out of that person. If it makes you feel more comfortable, find a perpetrator instead of a victim.

As soon as you can sense this person's energy being dislodged, mentally step in front of the Dragon's waiting mouth and claim this power as your own using the energy absorption method described above. Then follow this up with the steps for refining the energy in your stomach and then packing it in your Cauldron.

Next, try this same exercise in public. Go to a busy urban space and hang out until you encounter one or more persons being *looshed*.

Perhaps you'll overhear a heated argument at a cafe, or maybe you'll witness somebody being threatened by a bully. Rinse and repeat the energy absorption technique right then and there.

When and only when you're ready for a quantum leap in energy, this exercise can be expanded to include whole situations, small and large, of an unsavory or troublesome character.

You could have probably made yourself many thousands of Philosopher's Stones just by feeding on the tsunami of *loosh* waves unleashed by the Dragon through engineered events like the Twin Towers dog and pony show or JFK's magic-bullet assassination.

But even comparatively minor scenarios, such as a traffic jam with a fair amount of road rage or even a hotly contested sports event, can produce a significant *loosh* harvest.

Just be sure to rinse and repeat your technique with all its steps performed in order. Don't forget your Predatory Stance, an attitude that's actually beneficial to maintain throughout this process. And always remember to keep your tongue in proper position to limit the possibility of energetic overload.

If you ever have to postpone the energy packing phase because you're running out of time or circumstances around you are looking dicey, just make a note to carry that out as soon as you're in a more favorable position. In the meantime the energy can sit in your Cauldron, unpacked.

The ultimate test of your ability to absorb *loosh* in real time will come when you're able to practice the energy absorption technique in the middle of a conflict or argument *that you're personally participating in.*

To say this is challenging is an understatement. Nevertheless, endeavor to shut your mouth, quiet your mind, still your beating heart, and pull in the Dragon food bubbling out of you and the other concerned party or parties.

Keep doing this as long as you need to. Often, as I described earlier based on repeated personal experience, this will help resolve the situation … magically.

But even if it doesn't, you'll have gained additional personal power for your own use. Talk about taking lemons and making lemonade!

Energy Reabsorption

Now that you know how to absorb energy from your environment and circumstances in the now, you're ready to mentally project into your choice of a possible past or future and reabsorb power you've already lost there—time being, as a reminder, merely an absurdly profound illusion in which multiple so-called timelines exist simultaneously.

"The difference between energetic absorption in the present, as you judge the present using your physical senses," explains Kreiter, "and re-absorption in the past, is that you must go back to that past to do it."

Kreiter shares many considerations for projecting one's consciousness backward or forward. But to simplify things, just imagine that you're where you were or will be at the moment of losing some of your power.

Think of this as focusing your creative attention to make a past or future event—even a purely theoretical one or one that hasn't yet happened and may never happen to the you reading this—as mentally realistic as possible.

Such "real" and "fictitious" (note the lack of actual difference) events in our lives often involve trauma and strong emotions, both of which tend to lessen noticeably as you practice the energy reabsorption technique. So let's get to it!

Kreiter recommends performing this exercise in an enclosed space such as a closet in the manner of old-school shamanic recapitulation.

But honestly, I've found I'm a lot more comfortable and capable just lying in my bed with my sleeping mask on and earplugs in to shut out the present on my way into the past or future.

The main thing you want to avoid is falling asleep during reabsorption, since that negates the whole purpose. So if you need to sit or prop yourself up to keep from nodding off, by all means do so.

I like to perform this practice first thing in the morning, as it serves as a refreshing and empowering "meditation" that starts my day off on the right foot. But you can do it whenever you like—even just before bedtime or the middle of the night if the increased voltage doesn't wire you awake.

On that subject, as a quick aside, Kreiter shares that the "practice of energetic absorption and re-absorption naturally fortifies and increases the thickness, the gauge, of the body's wiring; which means that greater and greater amounts of energy can circulate around the body's circuits without a burnout. This extra energy also helps to increase the body's battery capacity."

Once you've arrived at the event you're planning to reabsorb energetically and can at least entertain the idea that you're actually there, simply perform the same steps we outlined for energy absorption—only this time applied to the nonlocal scenario taking place in an apparently different time.

A twenty-minute session is plenty. You may not want to do this every single day, as occasional mini-breaks can keep the process fresh. But the more often you perform this exercise, the more power you accumulate in your Cauldron, and the more healing on all levels you invite.

Consider beginning by reabsorbing any still unabsorbed negative events from the previous day, before transitioning to more distant memories. That way you keep from bailing out a sinking ship, as it were, by dying from a thousand new "*loosh* cuts" in your energy field even as you address more distant past or future ones.

An important and absolutely achievable goal is reabsorption of every bit of your lost energy and healing of any and all energetic wounds still bleeding your power even if they don't appear present.

As with shamanic recapitulation, it may be necessary to revisit stubborn traumas and reabsorb them multiple times. That's perfectly acceptable.

Beyond healing, of course, the larger goal is transformation (and ultimately transmutation) through creation of the Philosopher's Stone—a process greatly enhanced by adding reabsorption to your regular practice of absorption.

As your energy absorption and reabsorption continue over months and years, the more ordered your conscious mind becomes as the Dragon's operating system is gradually replaced by one it no longer controls.

This occurs owing to the fact that (re)acquiring, purifying and warehousing energy vastly magnifies your attention and ability to contain your emotional outbursts and resultant *loosh*. Eventually, the Great Parasite gives up trying to feed on you and leaves you alone.

Another way of innerstanding how reabsorption helps restore your right mind is to picture your foreign installation being repeatedly bathed in the unconscious realm of the Dark Sea of Awareness as you time travel—allowing the Father, alchemically speaking, to cleanse the Son and put the latter's thoughts in order.

The upshot is that practitioners tend to be burdened with less and less random internal dialogue while experiencing more and more inner quietude punctuated by meaningful and helpful thoughts of a largely creative and intuitive nature.

Disempowering the Dragon by Empowering Ourselves

There are a number of ways to expedite the process of generating your Philosopher's Stone.

One is to become a more powerful mental visualizer by following a specific protocol for progressing through the Seven Rooms (or what I like to call "Mental Chambers") of the Projectionist.

This is the mind-bending subject of the second and third books in Kreiter's trilogy, and it's also one I explore in an eminently practical way of my own devising in my PragmAlchemy series at **solluckman.substack.com**.

Becoming a more accomplished "projectionist" allows you to make the events you visit during your energy reabsorption sessions even more vivid and seemingly real, permitting you to more efficiently reintegrate lost power, which then increases your ability to project your consciousness … and so on and so forth in yet another absurdly profound ouroboros twist.

Additionally, Kreiter's first book in the trilogy relates another way of using your energy pumps in combination with reverse breathing, or what he calls "bone breathing," to facilitate greater energetic intake.

For the sake of clarity and so as not to overwhelm you, in this introductory text I've opted to stick to the basics. Here again, I offer my own simple but effective method for incorporating my own version of this technique in PragmAlchemy.

Rest assured that even with the tools I've provided here, you're well equipped to initiate your alchemical process of transmuting energy into true personal power that can eventually culminate—if applied with dedicated consistency—in the Philosopher's Stone.

As a fringe benefit for all and sundry, every morsel of power you personally ingest translates to less power going to the Dragon, which means your empowerment equates to its weakening. This occurs to some extent even with recapitulation, but as I've said, inner alchemy is far more to the point.

Imagine if the Matrix were populated by millions of inner alchemists instead of deluded optimists and useless pessimists.

Then, quite simply, the Dragon would no longer exist, at least not in the overbearing way it does now, and the Matrix would no longer be the Matrix but our very own world. And miracles would abound.

CHAPTER SEVENTEEN

Seal Your Fragmentary Body to Supercharge Your Energy Reacquisition

"[Potentiation] should be the starting place of every health practice. As a Naturopathic Medical Doctor and Acupuncturist, having a tool with which to align the body and create tangible potential for healing is beyond magnificent ... Anyone with a desire to elevate their energetic and physical potential needs to understand Luckman's work and experience it."
—Julie TwoMoon

Down the Rabbit Hole of Chronic Illness

Back in my twenties, prior to my Père Lachaise epiphany that led me to begin questioning the dogma surrounding mortality, I got seriously sick after opting for a series of recommended travel jabs on my way to perform dissertation research in South America.

Within a short period, I tumbled down the horrific rabbit hole of chronic illness. Virtually overnight, I found myself experiencing more food and environmental allergies than I could count.

These were paired with extreme chronic fatigue, an array of bizarre aches and pains like those described by fibromyalgia sufferers, and strange muscle twitches along with a kind of restless legs syndrome—to say nothing of dozens of other freakish symptoms that defied conventional medical diagnosis and treatment.

I spent tens of thousands of dollars I didn't have (being an impoverished grad student at the time) as I soldiered on into the bewildering world of holistic treatments. I tried everything from acupuncture and Transcendental Meditation to colon hydrotherapy and shamanic soul retrieval—but over the next few years, my condition only worsened.

Prior to Potentiation and the Regenetics Method, the only thing that actually helped somewhat, for any significant duration, was—surprise, surprise—*energy cultivation.* I learned a tremendous amount about this subject through direct personal experience by intensively practicing qigong for several years.

In case you're unfamiliar with it, qigong is a set of Taoist techniques for pooling and working with the life force, which is known as chi (sometimes spelled "qi").

When performed by practitioners who know what they're doing, qigong looks sort of like tai chi in super slow motion. In terms of the way qigong is designed to move chi around the body gracefully and elastically, I often thought of it as playing with etheric taffy.

Combining the balletic movements of qigong with the sexual inner alchemy aspect of this ancient practice (basically, a meditative abstinence allowing one to redirect libido for healing and other purposes), I was eventually able to get back on my feet—until a devastating series of root canals nearly finished off my immune system … and me along with it.

Discovering, or Rediscovering, the Fragmentary Body

As I detailed in my two books on the Regenetics Method, it was at this point that I encountered Dr. Devi Nambudripad's homeopathy-inspired Allergy Elimination Technique (NAET).

As a practitioner of a similar methodology derived from her work (which improved my health somewhat … until it stopped helping), I eventually acquired even more direct knowledge about our subtle anatomy and how hyperdimensional energy currents flow into and out of the body.

While performing many thousands of kinesiological assessments by muscle testing a large number of clients, I determined through my own repeated observation and experience that—almost universally—people suffer from a massive energy leak in the general region of the second (sex) *chakra*.

Additional research into esoteric and occult sources, including in-depth conversations with the leader of a well-known Egyptian Mystery School, led me to conclude that what I'm calling *the Fragmentary Body had been purposely hidden from the masses for the simple reason that it was a key to genuine awakening and empowerment.*

In light of our discussion of the Dragon's mimetic mind control of humans, whom it must keep ignorant in matters of true importance in order keep fat if not altogether happy on its worldwide *loosh* farm, it's understandable why the Fragmentary Body would have remained so long in obscurity.

Moreover, making sure its human herd had practically no clue as to the existence—much less any notion of what to do about—this still-open "Original Wound" (to use bestselling consciousness author David Wilcock's term) ensured that the Dragon would be able to extract the population's *loosh* almost effortlessly.

People's energy is constantly bleeding out through this rift in the biofield without their awareness. The pitiful state of modern humans' energy is a major theme in the works of Carlos Castaneda.

He basically asserts (I'm paraphrasing from memory) that the Mud Shadows—a Toltec name for Archons or the hive-minded Dragon—have fed on people until the auric energy of awareness that should be like great wings shining around them is trimmed practically all the way down below their ankles!

These days, however, more and more people are becoming aware of the Fragmentary Body—even if they address it with different language.

Though his understanding of this phenomenon is rather different from my own, renowned spiritual author Eckhart Tolle, for instance, famously called the Fragmentary Body the "pain body."

Bioenergy researcher Eileen Day McKusick, author of *Tuning the Human Biofield*, sees the Fragmentary Body much as I do. Having discovered this phenomenon independently through her own type of frequency mapping before reading my Regenetics books, which had already mapped it out, she called it the "slavery yoke."

To use an analog analogy, we can conceptualize the Fragmentary Body as a deep energetic scratch that keeps us in a narrow groove without access to the rest of the record of our totality.

Or to employ a term derived from Sanskrit, we might visualize this scratch as a negative *samskara*, a kind of mental rut that keeps human consciousness tracking through a limited and self-limiting Matrix of thought, feeling, and belief.

Thanks to the Dragon's serpentine trickery and our own desire to know more about ourselves, like Adam and Eve we were banished from knowledge (gnosis) of unity with the Dreamtime realm's Garden of Being.

The same force of duality that engendered the bifurcation of both our conscious and unconscious minds and our brains into left and right hemispheres simultaneously created the Fragmentary Body.

This was done, I propose, in order to energetically maintain the duality that characterizes our consciousness in a holding pattern—until we, individually for sure and maybe someday en masse, are ready to make contact with our inner Luminous Child, the Ghost in the Machine.

John Kreiter argues that this magical aspect of ourselves, thanks to its uncanny ability to bring together the conscious and unconscious minds, allows us to reunite the fragmented parts of ourselves in a far greater synthesis of our beingness than anything we've ever experienced … or even imagined.

Kreiter doesn't care much for the concept of "evolution." But if there's such a thing as evolution of consciousness, this is most assuredly it: the unification of the conscious mind (individuality) with the unconscious mind (unity) in a leapfrog "onward and upward" into a third state of consciousness that synthesizes in order to transcend both of them.

Truly, thanks to the intervention of our alchemical child, which is capable of unifying the conscious and unconscious aspects of our being, we can affirm that the whole of our identity is far, far greater than the sum of its parts!

To arrive at this whole, in my opinion, the Fragmentary Body *must* be addressed—one way or another.

This is the case because, as I explain in *Conscious Healing*, "the Fragmentary Body is an illusory—but no less powerful—dualistic principle of limitation that promotes disconnection from Source and, ultimately, death."

The Fragmentary Body & the Ghost in the Machine

It might be tempting to conflate the Fragmentary Body with the Ghost in the Machine. But while they're related, apparently having come into existence together when humanity "fell from grace" by accepting the Dragon's mind, they're not at all the same.

The Ghost is a byproduct (accidental or otherwise) of the installation of the Dragon's operating system, the conscious mind that suppressed humanity's far greater and more powerful unconscious mind.

The Fragmentary Body, on the other hand, appears to be the result of our new operating system's program, a "governor" of sorts that functions mechanically in true Archontic fashion to automatically control how much personal power people can store. In this way the Dragon's herd becomes less energized and more manageable.

Obviously, the above paragraph has a direct (and very serious) bearing on the first great goal of inner alchemy: creation of the Philosopher's Stone.

Repeated muscle testing located an extension of the Fragmentary Body just above the second *chakra*. In other words, an energetic protuberance was found below the third *chakra* just under the solar plexus and the Cauldron of inner alchemy.

But it gets worse. I've strongly intuited through my inner feeling sense based on personal experience and observation of thousands of clients that the Fragmentary Body—like a tapeworm placed in people by the Great Parasite—is designed to *pierce* the Cauldron from below and drain any excess energy that begins to build up there!

It goes without saying, then, if I'm right, that in order to create the Philosopher's Stone, the Fragmentary Body must be *removed*.

Fortunately, it can be. The method is actually quite simple. I've done it myself and helped countless others do it for themselves over the past two-plus decades.

Defragging the Body, Mind & Spirit

When one is fragmented, the only path forward is to defrag oneself, *duh*.

Thanks to ongoing kinesiological research, my partner, Leigh, and I weren't long in grasping that in order to heal one's divided bioenergy blueprint, it was necessary to go directly to our biology's interface with that blueprint: DNA.

In recent years there has been a lot of new information on, and strategies for dealing with, trauma—and for good reason. As I've argued in this book and my previous one, humans are a systematically traumatized species.

Past (and possibly even future) traumas tend to create energy blockages in the mind-body-spirit that limit the free flow of life energy, which is governed by DNA.

Think of the Fragmentary Body as our species' definitive traumatic event recorded in our biofield (aura)—and innerstand that the easiest, if perhaps not the only, way to defrag this fragmentation is to do so by activating the part of us that regulates the biofield: our genetics.

Thus my frequent use of the term *ener-genetic* to describe the symbiotic, reciprocal relationship between the bioenergy blueprint and DNA. One gives rise to the other, which gives rise to the other, ad infinitum.

Properly stimulated by sound and light, DNA can make changes to our energetic template. This blueprint can, in turn—like epigenetics but in a much more direct fashion—switch genes on and off to facilitate deep healing and transformation. Such altered DNA is capable of projecting a new and improved blueprint, which can then change genetic expression, which …

Yes, we're back to the absurdly profound, the circular ouroboros of our true nature that makes it so that we're forever giving birth … to ourselves.

Oh, No! Here Come the "Truthers" Again!

Over the past couple years, a sort of underground movement to dispute the existence—or at least, scientific proof of the reality—of DNA has started up among certain "truther" groups examining such thorny topics as virology and "scientism."

But having gone very far indeed down this particular rabbit hole also, my decades of research into the simulated nature of our so-called reality that I share in numerous books and articles ultimately led me to this question:

Is the scientific method broken—or did it never exist in the first place?

Upon careful consideration of the incredibly slippery nature of this "reality," where dozens of competing cosmological models show up even in mainstream science seemingly monthly, my position, as noted, is that *nothing really exists outside our own minds*.

Everything is made up by and with a single force focused by our attention to create the things we call things: the imagination.

Even our biological selves are constructs of consciousness, egregores, tulpas, avatars, fictional characters like my own self-imagining Luke Soloman brought to life by the exercise of personal and sometimes collective attention.

Viewed from this perspective, DNA represents not an extrinsic "real" but a kind of mutable mass agreement, culturally speaking, about who we consider ourselves to be biologically. And to that extent, DNA currently can be said to exist.

Science, such as it is, has indeed produced miracles: hybridization, cloning, etc. These amazing feats could be achieved because, as a people, we'd already dreamed the concept of DNA into existence and — unconsciously, let it be noted — accepted it as real.

Nothing — and I mean *nothing* — can be scientifically proven to absolutely and fundamentally exist. What's called science is, viewed from this angle, always and inevitably merely *scientism*.

When our "greatest minds" started trying to nail down matter, they entered the so-called atomic structure of things. From that moment researchers never stopped falling straight into the void of nothingness that is the Matrix.

The idea that DNA somehow "doesn't exist" because it was never "isolated" and "proven" is naively materialistic, a nitpicking observation made by a mind that doesn't innerstand the absurdly profound functionality of this at times maddening construct.

Rather than as a "real thing" outside ourselves, the world can be more productively conceptualized as a shared dream, an organic simulation dependent only on the "technology" of our shared imagination.

For practical purposes, however, we can approach the subject of DNA using the language of quantum bioholography. This is the study of DNA as a holographic, fractal phenomenon that, in essence, like the totality of ourselves, doesn't exist anywhere … yet it exists everywhere.

Using this model as conceptual scaffolding only, not as a universal "truth," we can speak about DNA as a holographic sound and light carrier wave that translates information between different octaves, dimensions, or areas of the construct.

If, for example, you experience trauma that then gets held in your biofield, it might express itself through the holographic translation mechanism that is DNA into different problems in your body, mind, or spirit.

Conversely, by activating DNA, it's possible to reverse this trauma—and even completely erase it from the bioenergy blueprint—thereby facilitating tangible, lasting resolution of health-related and other problems.

Such an ener-genetic approach to healing, or *wholing*, is the ultimate defrag—and it can work on everything from small traumas to the Grandaddy of Them All, the Fragmentary Body.

Seal Your Fragmentary Body with Potentiation

The first DNA activation in what eventually became the four-part Regenetics Method, Potentiation was the thing that finally corrected my autoimmune condition and gave me back my life.

And it did so in large measure, as I understood more and more over time watching so many clients experience similarly miraculous breakthroughs, by "deleting" the Fragmentary Body from my ener-genetic blueprint.

This isn't the place to go into fine detail about Potentiation and Regenetics. That would be impossible in a a single chapter. Practically every book I've ever written—fiction and nonfiction alike—touches on some aspect of this methodology that utterly altered the course of my life.

You can access all of that content (which even includes a recent video tutorial, *How to Potentiate Your DNA*, based on my book for performing your own or someone else's Potentiation) with a free trial at **solluckman.substack.com**.

To toot my own horn for a second, *Nexus* Magazine called Regenetics a "revolutionary healing science," a sentiment echoed in *New Dawn* Magazine's assessment of *Potentiate Your DNA* as "both fascinating and an astounding, perhaps even world-changing theory."

For now just know that this uniquely powerful form of sound healing prompts an integrated "reset" of the recipient's damaged or distorted biofield.

Interfacing with DNA to accomplish this feat, during which the old dualistic program of the Fragmentary Body is essentially overwritten, Potentiation uses sound and light waves. These are produced vocally and mentally through certain vowel pairings sung or chanted while keyed to a specific frequency, 528 hertz, generated using the "Mi" tuning fork from the ancient Solfeggio scale.

Dr. Leonard Horowitz has a lot to say about this singular frequency and the mysterious set of musical notes from which it derives. He calls "Mi" the "prosperity key of love" in his book with the same subtitle and considers this note unmatched in its ability to activate our innate potential for upgrading our lives in a multitude of ways.

An astonishing variety of benefits—physical, mental, emotional, and even spiritual—are regularly reported following Potentiation.

The greatest of these often occur after the sealing (deletion) of the Fragmentary Body, which happens approximately five months from the start of this activation—a process initiated, amazingly, by a *single* session that takes only *thirty* minutes and can be performed remotely for anyone anywhere.

As of the time of this writing, you can experience Potentiation absolutely free the first Sunday of every month, from wherever you are, with a Worldwide Potentiation Ceremony that Leigh and I personally perform. Visit **phoenixregenetics.org** to register.

Exit the *Loosh* Loop

In a world increasingly constructed out of mimetic desire as people become more and more connected inside the Dragon's net or web of technology, it should come as no surprise that memes are becoming a way of life.

Another meme I recently made, in relation to many of the ideas we've been discussing, featured these words: "Exit the *Loosh* Loop." I stand by all my suggestions for helping you do just that.

I encourage you to simplify your existence; explore the power of silence; find your groove again; get off your "truther" diet; do a digital detox; go off socials entirely from time to time; connect with the superpower of your uniqueness; procrastinate and moodle your way to creativity; and make peace with your shadow as you heed the call of your bliss and set out on your Hero's Journey.

I urge you to explore shamanic recapitulation as a means of recovering lost energy and reducing or eliminating past traumas.

And I wholeheartedly recommend delving into inner alchemy whenever you're ready to get to know your Ghost in the Machine while embarking on the creation of your own Philosopher's Stone.

But if I'm to be completely honest, at the risk of being accused of partiality, I must say that if I were to do one—and *only* one—thing mentioned in this book to shore up my energetic reserves and stop being a sitting duck for the Dragon and its minions to *loosh* at their leisure, I'd "potentiate" myself.

Not only did Potentiation literally save my life as it was being slowly and painfully leeched out of me for all to see; I've watched it improve other people's physical and mental health, and even lifestyle and relationships, in so many ways I lost count long ago.

Additionally, Potentiation can be done in conjunction with all the other strategies and techniques (including PragmAlchemy) I've mentioned herein—and it can make every last one of them a lot more effective.

Potentiation might not protect you from all types of energy loss to which you might be exposed. That said, correcting the primal dysfunction in your sex chakra is by far the fastest and most efficient way I know to gird up your loins for your ultimate battle against the Dragon as you push past it with your Ghost to continue your Hero's Journey beyond the *loosh* loop of the Matrix.

CHAPTER EIGHTEEN

Be a Rebel

"This is the end." —*Jim Morrison*

Which Road Do You Choose?

Here we are at the end of our road together, dear reader, and the beginning of your own road that leads … Where *does* your road lead?

This is a rhetorical question, obviously, and the possible answers are endless. But let's just say, for the sake of argument, that all roads go in one direction or another: backward into denial of the great mystery of existence or forward into delving ever deeper therein.

The first road leads to certain death and, eventually, as I understand it, loss of our individual consciousness as our particular energy signature is inexorably absorbed back into the Dark Sea of Awareness.

The second road, the one far less traveled, can take us to a multitude of marvelous places. But if we travel it long enough, it eventually leads to the same place—down to the shores of the Dark Sea.

Both roads lead to a definitive encounter with the end of our status quo: death.

The difference is that those arriving by the first road have no choice but to accept their fate in all its sobering finality, whereas those coming by the second road have one last trick up their sleeve.

To Pay or Not Pay the Ferryman?

In this book that began with a meditation on death in relation to rock 'n' roll, it seems only fitting that it should end that way as well.

Chris de Burgh's 1982 hit "Don't Pay the Ferryman" has intrigued listeners—yours truly included—for decades. The song tells the story of a man's encounter with the mythological figure of Charon from Greek mythology, the psychopomp responsible for ferrying the souls of the dead over the Acheron and Styx rivers that separate the realms of the living and deceased.

De Burgh's haunting lyrics relate the story of a man who apparently finds himself between these two worlds in an eerie riverside setting.

A deathly figure at the wheel of a riverboat shows up and offers to take him—for a fee, we're given to understand—to the far side. Grasping who's addressing him, the man refuses to pay the menacing ferryman and, in a most satisfying plot twist, appears to escape and run free.

"Don't Pay the Ferryman" wonderfully encapsulates the theme of the rebellious hero on his or her ultimate journey— the shaman, alchemist or psychonaut who has taken the second road to the water's edge and has no intention, to quote Dylan Thomas, of going "gentle into that good night."

Anteing up your small change as your final act is to give up your last bit of *loosh* and place the coins on your own eyes as they shut forever on your individual existence.

This is also the moment when the vast majority of souls sign their last and most depressing tacit yet binding contract with the Dragon that requires them to return to the Matrix *to do it all again*!

In this conclusive encounter with the Dragon's chief tax collector, so to speak, you either break free of the so-called reincarnation cycle complete with its memory wipe and the loss of individuality that entails—or you accept your fate, pay the ferryman his due, and get in line to be recycled back into this *loosh* farm not as yourself but as somebody else, again and again, until "you" figure out how to exit this funhouse for good.

Those who arrive at the Dark Sea by the first road always pay the ferryman. Having (to put it bluntly) wasted their time while squandering their vital force that might have been put to transcendent use, they have no other viable option.

But those rebels among us who have done their shadow and energetic work know that such payment is completely *optional*. For rebels death and taxes aren't the only certainties in life; for them there are *no* certainties. That's what makes it so exciting to be a rebel!

The choice whether to pay is entirely yours, but don't delay. Given the enormous amount of advance preparation required to not pay the ferryman, you might consider making your choice, like, *today*.

Inward, Outward & Onward

I couldn't think of a better way to end this book than with the following lyrics from one of my own rock songs. I trust you'll see what I mean.

May you get out of here alive—and may you experience a million miracles as your Hero's Journey takes you ever inward … and outward … then onward …

"Be a Rebel"

Some say we're in a trap
I'm down with that
But traps get a bad rap
When they're so much more than that

Be a rebel without a cause
Be a rebel without a clue
Be a rebel without a clue
Be a rebel just because
Do what you gotta do

Do what you gotta do

Do what you gotta do

What if there's an escape
What if there's an exit
What if you go in to escape
What if you go in to exit
In to exit

Rebel
A little devil
Stay disheveled

Feral and virile

Some say we're in a trap
I'm down with that
But traps get a bad rap
When they're so much more than that

Be a rebel without a cause
Be a rebel without a clue
Be a rebel just because
Do what you gotta do
Do what you gotta do

What if there's an escape
What if there's an exit
What if you go in to escape
What if you go in to exit
In to exit

Be a rebel without a cause
Be a rebel without a clue
Be a rebel just because
Do what you gotta do
Do what you gotta do

What if there's an escape

We're in a trap
I'm down with that
But traps get a bad rap
When they're so much more than that

Be a rebel without a cause
Be a rebel without a clue
Be a rebel without a cause
Be a rebel just because

Do what you gotta do
What you gotta do

What if there's an escape
What if there's an exit
What if you go in to escape
What if you go in to exit
In to exit

Be a rebel without a cause
Be a rebel without a clue
Be a rebel just because
Do what you gotta do
What you gotta do

What you gotta do

REVIEW

Sol Luckman here. Please accept my sincere thanks for being willing to give your precious attention to *Get Out of Here Alive*.

If you found value in this book and can spare a moment, I ask that you consider leaving a review on **Amazon.com**, **Goodreads.com**, **Bookbub.com** and/or other online book venues.

Reviews are the lifeblood of authors and their books, so know that your help here is greatly appreciated indeed!

Want to stay in the loop about new free content and other offerings from yours truly?

Join my mailing list:
https://solluckman.substack.com/subscribe

Browse my art portfolio:
https://sol-luckman.pixels.com

Subscribe to my YouTube:
https://www.youtube.com/@SolLuckmanUncensored

Follow me on Facebook/Meta:
https://www.facebook.com/solluckmanuncensored

Thank you again, dear reader, and may we soon meet again in the pages of another book!

BIBLIOGRAPHY & WEBOGRAPHY

Abelar, Taisha, *The Sorcerer's Crossing* (Compass, 1993)

Andrejkovics, Zoltan, *Together: AI & Human. On The Same Side.* (Independently published, 2019)

Author, Anonymous, *The Ripley Scroll: A Facsimile of the Pursuit for the Philosopher's Stone* (Erebus Society, 2018)

Barry, Lynda, *One Hundred Demons* (Drawn & Quarterly, 2005)

Baudrillard, Jean, *Simulacra & Simulation* (University of Michigan Press, 1994)

Blofeld, John, *The Tantric Mysticism of Tibet: A Practical Guide to the Theory, Purpose & Techniques of Tantric Meditation* (Penguin Books, 1992)

Cahalan, Susannah, "Why J. D. Salinger Was a Recluse" (*New York Post*, January 30, 2011)

Campbell, Joseph, *The Hero with a Thousand Faces (The Collected Works of Joseph Campbell)* (Joseph Campbell Foundation, 2020)

Castaneda, Carlos, *The Eagle's Gift* (Atria Books, 2013)
The Fire from Within (Atria Books, 2013)
The Journey to Ixtlan (Washington Square Press, 2012)
The Active Side of Infinity (Harper Perennial, 1999)
Magical Passes: The Practical Wisdom of the Shamans of Ancient Mexico (Harper Perennial, 1998)

Coelho, Paulo, *The Alchemist* (HarperOne, 2015)

Comer, John Mark, *The Ruthless Elimination of Hurry: How to Stay Emotionally Healthy & Spiritually Alive in the Chaos of the Modern World* (WaterBrook, 2019)

Dossey, Larry, "Why Consciousness Is Not the Brain" (https://snooze2awaken.com)

Eagle Feather, Ken, *Toltec Dreaming: Don Juan's Teachings on the Energy Body* (Bear & Company, 2007)

Fitzgerald, F. Scott, *The Crack-Up* (Alma Classics, 2018)

Frost, Robert, *The Poetry of Robert Frost: The Collected Poems* (Holt Paperbacks, 2002)

Galian, Laurence, *Alien Parasites: 40 Gnostic Truths to Defeat the Archon Invasion!* (Independently published, 2019)

Gibran, Kahlil, *The Prophet* (AB Books, 2023)

Girard, René, *Things Hidden since the Foundation of the World* (Stanford University Press, 1987)
Violence & the Sacred (Johns Hopkins University Press, 1979)

Goddard, Neville, *Your Faith Is Your Fortune (The Complete Neville Goddard Collection)* (Independently published, 2024)

Kerouac, Jack, *On the Road* (Penguin Books, 1976)

Harkness, Deborah, *A Discovery of Witches: A Novel* (Penguin Books, 2011)

Hawkins, David R., *Power vs. Force: The Hidden Determinants of Human Behavior* (Hay House, Inc., 1995)

Hopkins, Jerry & Sugerman, Danny, *No One Here Gets Out Alive* (Warner Books, 1995)

Horowitz, Leonard, *The Book of 528: Prosperity Key of Love* (Independently published, 2011)

Jung, Carl, *The Collected Works of C. G. Jung: Revised & Expanded Complete Digital Edition* (Princeton University Press, 2023)

Keats, John, *The Complete Works of John Keats: Poems, Plays & Personal Letters* (Musaicum Books, 2017)

Kelleher, Colm A., "Retrotransposons as Engines of Human Bodily Transformation" (*Journal of Scientific Exploration*, Spring 1999)

Kishimi, Ichiro & Koga, Fumitake, *The Courage to Be Disliked: The Japanese Phenomenon That Shows You How to Change Your Life & Achieve Real Happiness* (Atria Books, 2018)

Kreiter, John, *The Magnum Opus, A Step by Step Course* (Independently published, 2019)
The Way of the Projectionist: Alchemy's Secret Formula to Altered States & Breaking the Prison of the Flesh (Independently published, 2020)
The Way of the Death Defier: Apocryphon of Inner Alchemy (Independently published, 2021)

Kubler-Ross, Elisabeth, *Death: The Final Stage of Growth* (Scribner, 1997)

Larson, Dewey, *Beyond Space & Time* (North Pacific Publishers, 1995)

Lash, John Lamb, *Not in His Image: Gnostic Vision, Sacred Ecology & the Future of Belief* (Chelsea Green Publishing, 2021)

Levy, Paul, *Wetiko: Healing the Mind-Virus That Plagues Our World* (Inner Traditions, 2021)

Lipton, Bruce, *The Biology of Belief: Unleashing the Power of Consciousness, Matter & Miracles* (Hay House, 2016)

Lovecraft, H. P., *The Complete Fiction of H. P. Lovecraft* (Sanage Publishing House, 2021)

Luckman, Sol, *The World Cult & You: Your Place in It & Your Way Out of It* (Sol Luckman Uncensored, 2024)
Cali the Destroyer (Crow Rising Transformational Media, 2021)
Snooze: A Story of Awakening (Crow Rising Transformational Media, 2014)
Potentiate Your DNA: A Practical Guide to Healing & Transformation with the Regenetics Method (Crow Rising Transformational Media, 2011)
Conscious Healing: Book One on the Regenetics Method (Crow Rising Transformational Media, 2010)

Magaña, Sergio, *The Toltec Secret: Dreaming Practices of the Ancient Mexicans* (Hay House, 2014)

McKusick, Eileen Day, *Tuning the Human Biofield: Healing with Vibrational Sound* (Healing Arts Press, 2021)

Miller, Richard A., Webb, Burt & Dickson, Darden, "A Holographic Concept of Reality" (*Psychoenergetic Systems*, Vol. 1, 1975)

Mindell, Arnold, *Dreambody: The Body's Role in Revealing the Self* (Lao Tse Press, 1998)

Murphy, Brendan D., "Archons on Netflix? Gnostic Cosmology & Stranger Things Indeed" (https://solluckman.substack.com)

Montalk, Tom, *Transcending the Matrix Control System* (Independently published, 2023)

Morrison, Jim, *The Lords & the New Creatures* (Simon & Schuster, 1971)

Nambudripad, Devi, *Say Goodbye to Illness: A Revolutionary Treatment for Allergies & Allergy-Related Conditions* (Delta Publishing Co., 2016)

Namkhai Norbu, Chögyal, *Dream Yoga & the Practice of Natural Light* (Snow Lion, 1992)

Nietzsche, Friedrich, *Beyond Good & Evil: Prelude to a Philosophy of the Future* (Grapevine, 2019)

Orwell, George, *1984* (Global Publishers, 2024)

Phillips, Larry W., *Ernest Hemingway on Writing* (Scribner, 2002)

Pilgrim, Peace, *Peace Pilgrim: Her Life & Work in Her Own Words* (Ocean Tree Books, 1994)

Poe, Edgar Allan, *Edgar Allan Poe Macabre Tales & Poems* (Meijer, 2004)

Rappoport, Jon, "Are We Living in a Virtual Simulation?" (https://snooze2awaken.com)

Roth, Gabrielle, *Connections: Threads of Intuitive Wisdom* (Raven Recording, Inc., 2014)

Rowling, J. K., *Harry Potter & the Sorcerer's Stone* (Pottermore Publishing, 2015)

Ruiz, Don, & Mills, Janet, *The Mastery of Love: A Practical Guide to the Art of Relationship* (Amber-Allen Publishing, 2011)

Sheldrake, Rupert, *The Sense of Being Stared At: And Other Unexplained Powers of the Human Mind* (Park Street Press, 2013) "Morphic Resonance: Research & Papers" (https://www.sheldrake.org)

Thompson, Hunter S., *Fear & Loathing in Las Vegas: A Savage Journey to the Heart of the American Dream* (Vintage, 1998)

Thoreau, Henry David, *The Portable Thoreau* (Penguin Classics, 2012

Tolle, Eckhart, *The Power of Now: A Guide to Spiritual Enlightenment* (New World Library, 1999)

Ueland, Brenda, *If You Want to Write: A Book about Art, Independence & Spirit* (General Press, 2019)

Verne, Jules, *Jules Verne: Complete Works* (Wisehouse Classics, 2019)

Wilcock, David, *Divine Cosmos* (http://www.divinecosmos.com)

Yeats, W. B., *The Collected Poems of W. B. Yeats* (Scribner, 1996)

INDEX

U

Ueland, Brenda, 138–39
Undiscovered Country, 166, 173
unified field, 121
unity consciousness, 172
Universal Mind, 30

V

Vanlon Smith, Hendrith Jr., 130

W

waking world. *See* reality
Wedding Feast Parable, 151
weirdness, 89
wholeness, 165
wholing, 82
Wilcock, David, 210
withdrawal, 73

womb, 193, *See also* Cauldron
world. *See also* reality
    as projection of reality, 28
    as reflection of
        consciousness, 31
World Cult, 29, 126, 247
World Cult & You, xvi, 25, 80, 98,
    189, 247
world of the second attention.
    See second world
wu wei, *63–64*

Y

Yeats, W. B., 36

Z

Zahariades, Damon, 44

ABOUT THE AUTHOR

A polymath and modern-day Renaissance man, Sol Luckman has produced a wide variety of groundbreaking books across various genres—from international bestselling wellness nonfiction (*Potentiate Your DNA, Conscious Healing*) to multi-award-winning visionary fiction (*Cali the Destroyer, Snooze: A Story of Awakening*).

His extremely diverse works also include cutting-edge self-help (*Playing in the Magic, The World Cult & You*), artist memoir (*Musings from a Small Island*), and award-winning humor (*The Angel's Dictionary*).

This pioneering visual artist's colorful and emotive paintings have appeared on both mainstream and his own book covers. Recently, Sol has also released two full-length music albums (*Post-punk Shaman, Lost in a Sound Byte*) that lyrically develop numerous themes from his written work.

By embodying the potential to be more than just "another brick in the wall" of today's overcompartmentalized, niche-obsessed content creation landscape, Sol intends to lead by example—showing his readers that it's possible to think and succeed beyond artificial limitations in pursuit of authentic expression, personal sovereignty, and genuine wholeness.

Check out his website at **solluckman.substack.com**.

PragmAlchemy is Sol Luckman's new series of energy cultivation and self-bodywork exercises—and it's offered exclusively at solluckman.substack.com.

A hands-on, pragmatic approach to the often confusing and misleading discipline of inner alchemy, PragmAlchemy represents a major new addition to the esoteric **science of subtle energy cultivation**. Building up this life force is a no-brainer for anyone seeking to increase physical, mental or spiritual **health** as well as **longevity** and even the capacity for **manifestation**.

PragmAlchemy
WITH SOL LUCKMAN
Practical Energy &
Self-bodywork Strategies
for Wellness & Beyond

PragmAlchemy features an unmatched combination of deep myofascial release and targeted attention and breathing techniques for accumulating **life force**, purifying it, and condensing it for long-term storage.

The PragmAlchemy exercises are **DIY** all the way. None of them take longer than **ten-fifteen minutes** individually, though by combining two or more you can do longer sessions.

Some of the **many potential benefits** can include:

Increased mobility & flexibility	De-stressing
Greater core strength	Better moods
Tonification of organs	Higher energy levels
Productive detoxification	Heightened libido
Healthier digestion & elimination	Deeper sleep
Freer respiration	Rejuvenation
Help with pain	Inner calm
Hormone balancing	Clarity of purpose

Get started on your transmutational PragmAlchemy journey today at **solluckman.substack.com**.

Are you one of the few people living today who don't regularly give away their personal power to an established or clandestine cult?

Whether you answered "yes" or "no," you owe it to yourself to take the ultimate red pill that is *The World Cult & You* if you genuinely long to break free by innerstanding how this simulacrum of "reality" actually works.

Following in the footsteps of the great American philosopher and iconoclast Henry David Thoreau, award-winning and international bestselling author Sol Luckman levels a scintillating and sweeping social critique in this masterful examination of today's mass culture characterized by cults and cultishness at all levels.

Theorizing the existence of a World Cult divided into endless sub-cults all ultimately controlled by a spiritual adversary and designed to control humanity in turn, Luckman brilliantly blends simulation theory, quantum bioholography, lucid dreaming, Gnosticism, shamanism and philosophical skepticism to paint a sobering yet empowering picture of the consciousness landscape. You'll learn:

- ☑ How to identify your cults & cult handlers;

- ☑ A system for rating your own or another's degree of cultification;

- ☑ Who your greatest teacher is & why this matters;

- ☑ Strategies for taking back your energy & protecting yourself from the World Cult; &

- ☑ Tried-and-true techniques for building up personal power, with many practical, even tangible potential results.

Read the ebook or listen to the audiobook exclusively at **solluckman.substack.com**.

The first DNA activation in the "revolutionary healing science" (*Nexus*) of the Regenetics Method, Potentiation employs special linguistic codes—produced vocally and mentally—to stimulate a self-healing and transformational ability in DNA.

In this masterful exploration of sound healing by bestselling author Sol Luckman, learn how to activate your genetic potential—in a single 30-minute session!

Besides teaching you a leading-edge technique you can perform for your family, friends and even pets, *Potentiate Your DNA* also:

1. Provides a wealth of tested supplemental tools for maximizing your results; and

2. Outlines a pioneering theory linking genetics, energy and consciousness that is sure to inspire alternative and traditional healers alike.

Potentiate Your DNA "*is both fascinating and an astounding, perhaps even world-changing theory.*" —New Dawn *Magazine*

"Potentiate Your DNA *is brilliant and cutting-edge. Luckman has succinctly and elegantly provided a comprehensible intellectual framework for understanding the profound role of DNA in healing and transformation.*" —Brendan D. Murphy, author of The Grand Illusion

"*If you love the cutting-edge of the cutting-edge ... read this book!*" —Dr. David Kamnitzer

"*A gift of love, offering to all a simple, profound, elegant system of personal empowerment and self-healing.*" Carolyn Barnes, author of Return to Ease

Order the paperback, ebook or audiobook at **www.PhoenixRegenetics.org.**

The classic, definitive book on DNA activation, *Conscious Healing* is far more than the inspiring story of the development of a "revolutionary healing science that's expanding the boundaries of being" (*Nexus* Magazine).

An unparalleled synthesis of modern and ancient healing wisdom, this leading-edge text is essential reading for anyone interested in alternative medicine, energy healing, consciousness research, quantum biology, human evolution, or personal enlightenment.

Sol Luckman's bestselling, reader-friendly narrative details his experience of chronic illness and miraculous recovery thanks to the Regenetics Method of DNA activation—offering a ray of hope to those who, like the author, have "tried everything."

In addition, *Conscious Healing* provides scientific substantiation for the work of alternative healers from many orientations, clearly and convincingly making the case for energy work in general.

Order the paperback, ebook or audiobook at **www.PhoenixRegenetics.org.**

You know that excitement you get when a paranormal romance suddenly turns ... supernatural? Edgy, sexy and absolutely visionary, this one-of-a-kind love story will open eyes. The Goddess is afoot and things are about to get medieval in the Fatherland.

Patriarchal banking families with reptilian overlords, racial and sexual divisions, mass surveillance, social decadence ... Welcome to the future, after the 2nd American Revolution didn't go well.

What would happen if everyone suddenly woke up together and realized they were in an invisible prison run by psychopaths? In this amazingly uplifting dystopian thriller for young or old adults, experience the righting of the world in a future gone wrong.

Best friends? Check. Illegal lovers? Check. Mythological entities? Check.

Cali and Juice aren't discovering love; they're discovering they've always been in love—since the dawn of creation.

In this page-turner of a sci-fi tale set in an Orwellian future seeded in the dystopian present, resistance to the Archons appears futile ... that is, until the Goddess and her consort spectacularly reappear straight out of ancient Gnosticism to take on the control matrix of the Fatherland.

Will the Luminous Child awaken in humanity before it's too late?

"A thought-provoking and absorbing dystopian tale with a New Age touch [that] balances the exploration of human relationships with environmental, social, and political issues ... Cali the Destroyer *is an illuminating and deep read, and the result is a must-read tale in tune with contemporary concerns that it dresses up as an Orwellian future."* —Readers' Favorite

*"While [*Cali the Destroyer*] has plenty of laugh-out-loud scenes, it is also a cautionary tale. The Orwellian future Cali and Juice are familiar with may also be what ours looks like in several years.* Cali the Destroyer *shows readers what can happen when evil is allowed to thrive."* —Entrada Publishing

"Like some raconteur alchemist, Luckman comingles ancient mysticism, engaging characters, and social issues to sublimate the alchemical gold that is unique but timeless storytelling. As a dystopia, the work feels like it's happening right now. As a work of fiction, it feels like the perennial trope of man versus God— except it's hard to tell who the villain or hero is. A simultaneously disturbing and amazing read, you'll probably end up finding your own Philosopher's Stone." —Miguel Conner, Author, Voices of Gnosticism & Host, Aeon Byte Gnostic Radio

Purchase the paperback, ebook or audiobook at **www.CrowRising.com.**

Could it be there's no such thing as the paranormal ... only infinite varieties of normal we've yet to understand?

From acclaimed author Sol Luckman comes *Snooze*, the riveting tale of one extraordinary boy's awakening to the world-changing reality of his dreams, winner of the 2015 National Indie Excellence Award for New Age Fiction and 2016 Readers' Favorite International Book Award Finalist in the Young Adult-Coming of Age category.

Join Max Diver, aka "Snooze," along the razor's edge of a quest to rescue his astronaut father from a fate stranger than death in the exotic, perilous Otherworld of sleep.

An insightful look at a plethora of paranormal subjects, from Sasquatch and lucid dreaming to time travel via the Bermuda Triangle, *Snooze* also shines as a work of literature featuring indelible characters, intense drama and breathless pacing to stir you wide awake!

"Luckman's dazzling abilities as a novelist abound with lyrical prose ... If you enjoy colorful characters, a fast-paced plot and stories that tug at your heart, this novel in eighty-four chapters is anything but a yawn." —Readers' Favorite

"A multi-dimensional, many-faceted gem of a read. From mysteries to metaphysics, entering the dream world, bigfoot, high magic and daring feats of courage, this book has it all." —Lance White, Author of Tales of a Zany Mystic

"A book for readers ready to awaken from our mass cultural illusion before we self-destruct. Snooze calls out for readers open to the challenging adventure of opening their minds." —Merry Hall, Co-Host of Envision This

Purchase the paperback, ebook or audiobook at **www.CrowRising.com.**

Made in United States
Orlando, FL
28 March 2025

59933619R00148